HOW TO TRAIN
OPTIMISTIC
MIND

BUILDING EMOTIONAL
RESILIENCE IN A TROUBLED WORLD

MARINA LANDO

HOW TO TRAIN OPTIMISTIC MIND

Building Emotional Resilience in a Troubled World

ISBN: 979-8-9857302-0-3

Cover and Book Design by
Transcendent Publishing

TRANSCENDENT
publishing

Printed in the United States of America.

DEDICATION

To my grandmother Stanislava and my parents Emma and Emmik, who taught me that the light is inside me, not outside.

"Freedom is what you do with what's
been done to you."

Jean-Paul Sartre

TABLE OF CONTENTS

ACKNOWLEDGMENTS

I would like to thank Jennifer Henderson for editing this book and going through it with a fine-tooth comb, and for suggesting a quote by Maya Angelou.

I would also like to give a big thank you to all my clients and students. You thought I was teaching you. But you were also teaching me. I could not have written this book without you!

1

STOP SHORTENING YOUR LIFESPAN

Most books start with an introduction. I am skipping this time-honored tradition and will cut to the chase. The clock is ticking and neither you nor I have the luxury of limitless time.

Let me ask you a simple question. Would you be willing to live in the house of a hoarder? Odds are, you already do.

Most people take good care of themselves and their families. You are not an exception. You try to exercise regularly, eat right, sleep at least seven hours each night, and drink plenty of water. Excellent!

But what about your inner peace? What about your happiness? Your inner balance? You spend most of your time worrying about this and that, working yourself into a frenzy about future outcomes, and brooding about past mistakes. All of this emotional effort takes time you don't have the luxury to waste nor any way to replenish.

Compare your body to a house. It appears you take good care of the walls and foundation. You keep yourself busy between the gym, a hairdresser appointment, shopping for the latest in styles and beauty care. All these frantic activities, all these efforts to look perfect, your constant desire to be up-to-date on all the news and social media posts, not to mention all those text messages and emails—you rarely have time for the most important part of your life. For you.

The outside of your house may be stunning and spark envy in neighbors and social media followers. But inside is complete chaos. Old heartbreaks are heaped into a closet, and you cannot even shut the door. Anger decays in the kitchen sink, poisoning the air. All the grudges you ever had are piled in stacks to the ceiling, threatening to collapse with the slightest movement of the air. Inside your house, it is so crammed and crowded you can barely move.

Would you willingly live in the house of a hoarder? Probably not. So why do you force your mind to live in one?

You were born with optimistic mind. Your "house" might have appeared shaky from the outside, but inside it was clean and full of light. It was a perfect house for your mind. Your mind was happy inside this house, ready to experience the world and savor many adventures. You had optimistic mind. However, as time has passed and old unresolved issues have accumulated, they not only have created unnecessary pain and suffering; they have prevented you from achieving your goals.

Optimistic mind grows and thrives. To the pessimistic mind, the world appears full of danger, void of opportunity, and loveless. Pessimistic mind traps you in a perpetual loop of misery.

You can achieve your full potential only when you cultivate optimistic mind. Optimistic mind always moves forward, always looks for solutions, always opens to love and compassion.

Did you ever try to drive to a grocery store in a broken car? This might be an exciting journey and provide a good story to tell, but the trip would take three hours instead of ten minutes. The two hours and fifty minutes you lost cannot be purchased, renegotiated, or borrowed. They are gone. So how do you plan to achieve your dreams with an exhausted and burned-out self? Don't make yourself into a good dramatic story to tell. That is not why you are here. You are here to make the world a better place. You are here to make someone very happy.

Pessimistic mind interrupts the flow of your thoughts and interferes with your decisions. It effectively shortens your active life span and makes you spend your time on things that neither matter nor help you achieve your goals. For example, imagine yourself driving to work thinking about a new project, and you come up with an amazing, elegant, and simple solution. You are so excited and happy. The idea needs polishing but... suddenly, out of the blue, someone cuts you off. The adrenaline rushes through your body, you demonstrate extraordinary defensive driving abilities, you avoid a dangerous accident, and you save lives. You will arrive on time for the important meeting, and you will have a car to drive your child to football practice in the evening. Great job!

But you are fuming with anger and full of rage and indignation. You curse, you spend time comparing your perfect driving to that of this moron, you feel upset. You contemplate why you were a target of such an atrocity. And, now that you think about it, wasn't your ex also a horrible driver? Now you feel hatred towards your ex and the driver. You arrive to work, where you will spend an additional thirty minutes venting your frustration about bad driving to co-workers. You were so happy before that stupid driver interfered with your life and ruined your day. Yes, you had such happy thoughts. . . . What were you thinking about? Something about your project. Well... those thoughts are gone. Maybe they will come to you later, or maybe they won't.

One of the few things you cannot buy in this life is extra time. And you just spent an hour of your valuable life for what? And that perfect idea, the solution to your work problem, is gone, buried under the rubble of your anger. If you could just avoid the collision and keep thinking about your project without enduring all these tribulations caused by anger, you will achieve much more in your life. The world will be a better place and you will feel happier. And if you could avoid being played by pessimistic mind, you would not snap at your child for being two minutes late to drive to football practice.

It is possible to escape the trap of pessimistic mind when you know how to train and build your optimistic mind. In the chapters that follow, I will teach you how to unleash these powers, which already exist within you.

Let us look at some numbers.

When you are born, you can expect to live about 80 years. Good. You have many wonderful things to achieve.

You will spend 26 years sleeping. So, you are left with 54 years of active life. Still a very good number.

Sociologists say that on average you will spend 5 years worrying, 4 years angry, 6 years envying, 5 years feeling lonely, and 5 years in fear. So, you are left with 29 years. But if you also take into consideration: anxiety, doubts, attachment, insecurity, frustration, and so forth—roughly 3 years each—you will realize you don't have much active useful life left. If you don't know how to use the energy of emotions in a productive—instead of a destructive—way, you might never achieve your full potential.

What about your personal life? Unfortunately, pessimistic mind plays a devastating role in your intimate relationships. Pessimistic mind is insecure, eager to judge, and experiences extreme jealousy. Pessimistic mind can leave you vulnerable to abuse or can make you a cynic, unable to create deep, meaningful relationships. It makes dating such a nightmare for many. Optimistic mind just coolly moves on until you find The One.

In plain English: pessimistic mind creates an intricate obstacle course between you and your objectives. Why waste your time jumping through hoops when you can just walk towards your dreams?

What are your dreams? A better job, a better family, a better world, or a better you? You can achieve nothing if you are busy trying to ignore or cover your emotions. Attempting to hide unhappiness or a burn-out takes too much energy. If you are too busy and too tired, how can you achieve your dreams?

Have you tried self-help books? How many? Did they work?

2

WHY SELF-HELP BOOKS DON'T WORK

Do you ever wonder why you can't be your very best no matter how many self-improvement books you read, how many motivational seminars you attend, or how many task management apps you have on your very smart phone?

I know. It's a bummer.

My Facebook feed is full of good-intentioned quotes posted by well-intentioned people. We like to share these uplifting quotes to "manifest" one thing or another. I believe it works as well as good old-fashioned chain letters. Remember those? "Send this letter to ten of your friends to get good fortune in the next week." The only institution doing well was the post office.

Oh, the joys of self-sabotage! What happened to our best intentions to

- start this…
- stop that…
- finally finish….

You need look no farther than your mind. Everything you need is all there.

Pessimistic mind triggers strange responses and makes decisions for you. In retrospect some decisions seem irrational, but neither you nor your pessimistic mind can fully understand how you came to these surprising conclusions. With pessimistic mind in control, you are stuck in a negative and repetitious loop.

How many times have you tried to start looking for a new job, begin a diet, or go to the gym? Why is it always next Monday? Sound familiar?

According to Ayurveda, a five-thousand-year-old very complex holistic medical system from India, our body metabolizes food, water, air, and emotions. If one of these elements is "hard to digest," you become sick. When you stop processing your emotions and start sweeping them inside the house, they create pessimistic mind.

How does this happen? Every minute you experience life through a constant flow of emotions. Emotions are just energies (called Prana in Ayurveda) you absorb via marmas, points on your skin similar in nature to acupuncture points. Under normal conditions you recognize emotions and let your body process them. Nothing to write home about. Only when you experience a shock, or are under a lot of pressure, or don't want to look or act like a bad person or a coward, can emotions become toxic. Toxic emotion creates a micro-PTSD and builds pessimistic mind.

When emotions you experience become too much to bear, your untrained mind recoils. You push emotions away, you try to fight them, to forget them, you don't allow your body to process them. "I cannot feel that...", "This is not happening...", "I am going to explode...". You close the points where the energy of emotions is channeled into your body and stop processing these energies. Your body, deprived of needed energy flow, develops diseases. For example, unprocessed anger can cause liver problems.

Your mind shifts from optimistic to pessimistic and your mental state from balanced and happy to gloomy. Unprocessed emotions cause a lot of misery and frustration. They create the illusion that powers you possess are outside of your control and out of your reach. When you don't process the emotion of anger, you are not less but even more angry and irritable. Now even small things make you mad. These small things become big things that "intentionally" make you miserable and prevent you from achieving happiness and your goals. People driving their cars in a way you consider inconvenient or food at a restaurant not prepared exactly to your standards can ruin your entire perfectly planned day. Or perhaps you find yourself in hopeless circumstances. If any of this sounds familiar to you, it is a warning that toxic emotions have made your mind pessimistic. Don't despair: there is always a solution.

Pessimistic mind doesn't make you weak or bad. You are just wounded. This book will teach you how to use ancient proven techniques to heal those wounds, build optimistic mind, and achieve happiness and productivity.

Pessimistic mind might trigger pain, disease, intense reactions to insignificant events, or even phobias. It makes you feel unfulfilled, bitter, and disillusioned. In extreme cases your mind becomes so wounded, gloomy, and biased you try to run away from it. You become a self you want to forget. Pessimistic mind can make you crave alcohol, drugs, food, or gambling. Anything to feel happy again.

Pessimistic mind makes you feel perpetually incomplete and insecure. This sense of lost control forces you to try to find external props. You may have urges for shopping sprees for the latest fashion, a new car, the most advanced gadgets. Other types of props may be less material: a new miracle diet craze, a new exercise, or even a new religion or political movement. Companies and politicians know how to manipulate people with pessimistic mind by offering them props in the form of goods, services, and political promises.

Processed emotions reinforce your optimistic mind and bring you a sense of confidence, pride, purpose, and hope. Optimistic mind is rational, creative, and calm. It makes you open-minded to new experiences, new people, and new ideas.

Optimistic mind is kind and nonjudgmental. Optimists attract people and have an easy time promoting new ideas and making friends. Optimists may try a lot of things and make a lot of mistakes, but they gain wisdom. This wisdom is a solid foundation for success in personal and professional life. Optimists cannot be seduced by fame or power because they don't need external props to feel secure and fulfilled. Optimists can find solutions in the most difficult circumstances. Optimists are always in control.

Pessimistic mind makes you miss opportunities. Pessimists might make fewer mistakes, but they will not gain the wisdom necessary for success. Pessimists are frustrated with themselves and the world. To feel important, they are judgmental and criticize people, events, and ideas. Because of constant negativity, pessimists cannot attract balanced people and have difficulty keeping projects on track or finding suitable partners. Pessimists cannot find solutions and blame unfavorable circumstances or enemies for their own mistakes. Pessimists are vulnerable to manipulation by companies and other people and to emotional and physical abuse in personal and professional life.

Pessimistic mind makes you think you have lost control. Frustration will build up to the boiling point when you start seeking external tools to get your control back. When the power appears to be outside of you and out of your reach, pessimistic mind blames the world and seeks external powers to fix things.

The same applies to relationships. Feeling unhappy, pessimistic mind will search for happiness outside of the current relationship. The truth is no one can make you happy but you. But pessimistic mind will push you towards partners who find satisfaction in manipulation, not partners who complete you. You will be used, not cherished for who you truly are.

When you become fluent in processing emotions, you build optimistic mind, reclaim your inner powers, and gain control of your life. The energies of emotions propel your ideas and your talents toward changing the world. You become a confident, balanced person who attracts strong partners and enters long-lasting relationships in love and friendship.

Pessimistic mind makes you a victim. Optimistic mind makes you a hero. A victim gives up. A hero rises above all challenges and is rewarded. A victim doesn't see the way out. A hero finds the solution. Are you a hero or a victim? It is your choice. It is all inside you.

This book will give you the knowledge and tools to train and rebuild optimistic mind and start every day refreshed and ready for the fascinating challenges life brings. Use these tools well.

3

TOXIC EMOTIONS AND THE DISTRACTION OF THE OPTIMISTIC MIND

In a single day you experience a myriad of emotions. There is never a dull moment while you are awake (or asleep, for that matter). Our day starts and ends with emotions.

Wake-up: anxiety about today's meeting. Brushing teeth: shame about extra cushions of fat on your belly. Breakfast: anger over Facebook post. In a car: pure rage over that guy who did not stop at the red light. At work: panic over your project deadline. After work: insecurity over a personal relationship. The next morning: anxiety about today's meeting. And on, and on, and on....

To top it all: you are ashamed and angry for feeling angry and ashamed all the time. You are afraid to show your "weaknesses" and your emotions to others.

To "cure" this situation, you sweep every shameful and bad emotion inside the house until there is no space to move, and no light comes from outside. You are constantly bumping into the shaky towers of old memories and unprocessed emotions, sending them roaring down on your unprotected head. You experience emotional pain and waste a great deal of time digging yourself out of the hole again. And again… and again….

But what if there is an easier, more pleasant way to experience life? Actually, the easy part requires a lot of work.

There is no pleasure in suffering. Suffering does not achieve anything. It doesn't make you more productive or a better person.

Remember: your life is not a test. It is a journey. Calamities, heartbreaks, and disease are not curses or punishments. Things just happen all the time to everyone. In many cases the way you react to events makes them a passing incident or a life-altering catastrophe.

4

PER ASPERA AD ASTRA (THROUGH HARDSHIPS TO THE STARS)

Once someone said to me, "I want to be you."

"You definitely don't want to be me," I replied.

I was badly bullied at school by classmates and teachers for a simple accident of birth. My father is Jewish. This was a huge detriment in the Soviet Union Paradise where everyone was equal. Some were less equal than others, however. From early on, I learned to be angry.

While teenagers in the West were learning about the opportunities of college education and how their talents could lead to gainful employment, I was learning my limitations (largely because of my Jewish father). I learned not to dream of the unachievable. I learned that I couldn't be a doctor, a writer, or a journalist.

I lived through the Chernobyl disaster and learned to stay indoors, to stop dancing under the summer rain, and to fear the northern winds.

I lived through the last attempt of the Communist Party to seize power and overthrow a legally elected government and I learned to be desperate.

I lived through the disintegration of the Soviet Union and total collapse of all infrastructure. I learned to be hungry.

I lived through immigration. My family of 5 and our dog came to the United States with six hundred dollars, and I learned to be insecure.

I lived through the loss of an unborn child and the sudden unexpected death of my husband of twenty-five years, and I learned grief.

However, through all these unfortunate events, I learned great lessons. I learned to forgive, I learned the meaning of dedication, I learned to be kind, I learned to be brave, I learned how to change.

But you do not want to be me. You might not believe it, but you are here to change the world for the better and make people happy.

There are no insignificant lives. I don't know you. But what I know for sure is that you picked up this book because you are a fighter. In your life you experienced your own great disasters. It might be rape, betrayal, death, loss, injustice, disease, or discrimination. But you are not a sissy. You did not choose to give up, to drink yourself into oblivion, or to overdose. You chose to learn. You might just have gotten a blow to the gut. You might be on the floor howling.

Get up! Get up and live! There is a way to win your battles, there is a way to be kind, there is a way to be you and to make the most of your life in any circumstances.

Many people confuse "the survival of the fittest" for "survival of the meanest." This is the illusion of pessimistic mind. History and experience teach us otherwise. Families, communities, and countries survive because of acts of kindness. Because communities come together to protect the vulnerable and injured. The world survives and moves forward because of optimistic mind and its kindness.

Compassion saves the world from destruction. And the first thing you must learn is compassion towards yourself. I will show you how you can gain a deeper understanding of your reaction to the events around you and acquire tools to build emotional resilience. You will learn how to teach yourself to be the more content, happier, and satisfied person you always dreamed you could be. How to be a person everyone wants to have as a friend, as a spouse, as a co-worker, as a parent. Shall we begin?

5

GOOD EMOTION VS. BAD EMOTION

Emotions are your birthright. Experience triggers emotions. There is no way around it—you are designed this way. It is in your DNA. Emotions are not there to challenge or cripple you. They are there for a purpose. Emotion is the protective response of an energetic body to the situation at hand. You might call it the emotional immune response.

Being ashamed that you experience fear is as useless and counterproductive as being ashamed of having a fever when you have a cold or the flu. Fever helps your body deal with infections. Fear helps you to deal with dangerous situations.

Emotions help you to solve your everyday predicaments. Grief to heal your broken heart, fear to save yourself, envy for self-improvement. When you start looking at emotions from the constructive point of view, they make more sense.

Experiencing emotions does not make you good or bad. You are entitled to experience the full range of emotions, from anger to happiness and all shades in between. Emotions make you human. Only what you do with the energy of emotions makes you moral or immoral. Don't worry, however, you obviously want to be a good person. The best part: you are always in control. It is our choices that make us good or bad, not our emotions.

I love this old Buddhist story about a teacher and his student. The teacher noticed that his student looked troubled, with dark circles under his eyes from lack of sleep. "What is happening?" asked the teacher. "Do you sleep well? I noticed you did not touch your breakfast. You have to nourish your body, not just your soul."

"Oh, dear Teacher," said the student. "I am not well. Not well at all. I think I am not worthy to study Buddhism with you anymore. I have to leave."

"But why?" asked the teacher.

"Every night I have this terrible dream. There are two dragons. The white one represents everything that is good in me and the black one represents everything that is evil in me. And they fight for my soul. I am so anxious which dragon will win and so horrified that the black dragon will win that I wake up. If I were a good person this dream would never happen."

"Don't worry, my student," said the teacher. "The important part is not who is going to win, but who YOU want to win. The dragon you want to win WILL win."

It is you and only you who decides how to use your emotions. You and only you decide which dragon will win. You and only you make a choice between pessimistic and optimistic mind.

Accepting an emotion is nothing to write home about (or should I say, nothing to post on Facebook about). Only when you block the emotion do you get into trouble. When feelings become toxic, they create emotional imbalance and nourish the pessimistic mind.

Emotions are just energies. Each has a different flavor. You and only you decide what to do with the energy of emotion. When you permit your body to accept the emotion, you utilize the full power of energies you need to survive and build optimistic mind.

The purpose of anxiety, for example, is not to paralyze us but to amplify all our senses. To help us evaluate a situation for dangers and make a cool-headed decision.

Use it and diffuse it. Block it and it leads to suffering.

We judge our emotions. Compassion is a "good" emotion, anger is a "bad" emotion, fear is not "good" or "bad," just too intense. When you block an emotion, you think you don't experience it anymore. But it is there, a ticking time bomb. It is difficult to see the cause of the problem when you have developed pessimistic mind.

In the pages that follow, you will learn how to utilize simple ancient techniques used by Buddhist monks for centuries to balance emotions and cultivate optimistic mind. And how to use the powerful energy of all your emotions to create the life you have always wanted.

6

HOW TO USE THIS BOOK EFFICIENTLY

I first developed this program in 2011. Since then, I have helped hundreds of my clients realize their full potential in their personal and professional lives. My clients achieved something they thought was beyond their reach: built families, created successful businesses, and published books.

This book is the result of many hours of research and practical application to the most complicated cases.

Read Chapters "Free Meditations and Resources" through "Nurturing Optimistic Mind" first. Become familiar with the tools.

6.1 Free Meditations

I have recorded guided meditations for each emotion described in this book and created How to Train Optimistic Mind Book Companion.

Get these valuable tools for free at Lando Medical Reiki Academy:

1. Go to https://lando-medical-reiki-academy.thinkific.com/
2. Click on "Book Companion"

3. Click on "How to Train Optimistic Mind Book Companion"
4. Click "Buy" to add it to your cart
5. Enter the code **o4timist1c** and get all meditations for this book for free.

And practice, practice, practice. Practice makes perfect. Meditate daily. Five minutes a day is all that it takes to make you strong, resilient, and happy.

I recommend working with each emotion in the order they are listed in this book and following the weekly plans. Don't rush through it. This book is meant for very slow and thoughtful reading. One chapter a week is all you need. A reading meditation. Following the provided weekly plan will give you the most benefits.

Eventually you will start recognizing when you don't process emotion properly and working with that emotion as soon as you can find a quiet place to meditate. This is how you will build your emotional resilience and optimistic mind.

7

WHAT IS DOSHA?

Let's start with a very short course on doshas. *Dosha* is a Sanskrit word and means "constitution." Your constitution determines how you react to events around you.

Ayurveda recognizes three Doshas: Vata, Pitta, and Kapha. As in traditional Chinese medicine, Ayurveda recognizes five basic elements: space (as distance), air, water, fire, and earth.

Each Dosha is a combination of two elements.

Vata is a combination of space and air. In a balanced state, Vata people are very creative. Out of balance, they are disorganized and feel very chaotic.

Pitta is a combination of water and fire. In a balanced state, Pitta people are very productive. They are also good leaders. Out of balance, they are very angry and impatient.

Kapha is a combination of water and earth. In a balanced state, Kapha people are very loving and caring. Out of balance they become melancholic and depressed.

Did you recognize yourself? Sometimes when I get very mad, I tell myself: "It is ok. My Pitta is out of balance. Let's meditate."

Toxic emotions can bring doshas out of balance. When you release and process toxic emotions, you balance doshas and nourish optimistic mind. Balanced doshas will gradually help balance your body, and optimistic mind will help you build the life you deserve.

8

MEDITATION

"Forgive yourself for not knowing what you didn't know
before you learned it."

Maya Angelou

To help to release the blockage, you will be using ancient Tonglen
meditation. Tonglen meditation is a practice that originated in Tibet
almost a thousand years ago. Tonglen has many applications. You can
listen to different teachings on this meditation for years and never hear
the same application of this wonderful practice. It is a very effective
meditation and always my first choice to work with toxic emotions.

There are many hours of teachings about this practice. For our purpose
I shortened the teaching into these three simple steps.

8.1 Step One

In step one you will learn to accept your emotions as a part of you. No one
imposes emotions on you. You are the one who experiences emotions.
Emotions are just energies to help you to deal with your life. During the

day you experience a constant flow of emotions—some pleasant, some painful. You must accept them all without punishing yourself and without judging yourself for experiencing them. Emotions are neither good nor bad. It is your birthright to experience a full spectrum of emotions, from happiness to anger. Only you can make an emotion good or bad, because only you can choose the way it will be used. According to Ayurveda, emotions are just flavors of energy that flow through you. These energies feed our organs and tissues and help them to respond and function. They exist to help us deal with the situation at hand. Think about emotions as the immune response of your energy field. You cannot get angry at yourself because you have a fever. Fever kills infections.

You see, it is our choices. It is always our choices. And it is in your power to train your mind to be optimistic. And if changing the world is not your dream, at least you will feel better.

In step one you must accept your own emotions with compassion. I must warn you: It is easier said than done. All of us enjoy nagging and judging ourselves tremendously. It is hard to break an addiction.

Compassion is unconditional love. But what is the meaning of "unconditional"?

It means:

- Without judgment
- Without punishment
- With patience
- Without any expectations

To help you understand, let me tell you a story.

Imagine yourself driving a car on a highway and suddenly you see a little animal on the road. You stop the car and make sure you are safe and will not be hit by other cars. You get out of the car and find a little two-month-old kitten. You pick her up and take her back to the farm, from which she obviously escaped, far from the road so she will not be killed.

Ask yourself a few simple questions (make sure you actually answer each question before moving to the next one):

- Did you judge the kitten for being on the road?
- Did you punish the kitten for being on the road?
- Were you patient with the kitten?
- Do you expect that the kitten will never wander onto a road again?

When I ask my clients these questions they start smiling. I see you smile, too. Of course, it is ridiculous to judge a little kitten for being on the road. Kittens are cute and innocent, and they have no instincts about a road or its dangers. You cannot punish any kitten for being on a road. They never wander on a road because of some "catspiracy." They just don't know better. They have no experience and no wisdom. Of course, everyone would be very patient with the kitten, so it will not get scared. And never has even a single person told me that they expected the kitten to learn the "road equals danger" rule from that very first experience.

I want you to pause and think about it. Now answer me: why are you so compassionate towards a kitten you have never seen before in your life, a complete unknown creature, you don't even know its parents or the owner, but you cannot be compassionate towards yourself? I want to know the answer. And I am sure you want to know the answer, too.

Were you born with a degree in any science or liberal arts? No? Were you born as an expert in human communication? No. At the time of your birth you cannot even speak your mother's language!

What is my point? It is this: you learn as you grow. You continue to learn as you become old. It never ends. No one taught me to be a mother. I learned it. Every day I learned a new set of skills and the next day they became obsolete. I learned how to be a mother to a newborn, to a toddler, to a teenager. And now I am learning how to be a mother to a grown man. I made mistakes, I learned from them, and I moved on to new mistakes.

We all learn how to be a child, a friend, a human, a lover, a spouse, a parent, a stranger, a widow, a grandparent. None of us know how to do it. And it is OK. We all make mistakes. And you are entitled to make mistakes, too. Mistakes are lessons; without them you cannot learn. Mistakes give you wisdom. Wisdom brings you success. But only optimistic mind can recognize a lesson in a mistake and gain wisdom.

Life is a journey, not a test. You cannot judge yourself for not know-ing what you have not learned. You cannot punish yourself for not knowing a lesson you have not yet been given. You must learn to be patient with yourself. You cannot expect any immediate result. Learn-ing takes time and many lessons. Think about yourself as a vulnerable and innocent kitten if it helps.

8.2 Step Two

In step two you become aware that you are surrounded by people who make the same mistakes you do, experience the same emotions you do, and suffer from these emotions the same way you do. All of us. No exceptions.

Let's make it clear: all humans experience emotions in the same way. It would be impossible for us to create a civilization or any form of society without sharing not just biological similarities but also similar emotional responses. Our society is built on human communication, and it would be impossible to interact if we did not have the same emotional reactions. Can you imagine telling your friends that you just had a very bad breakup with a long-time significant other and they start to laugh? No, because your friends understand the emotional pain you experience. They can relate. They have had similar experiences, similar emotions, similar sufferings.

When we experience a painful emotion, we all suffer from it in the same way and at the same level. There is no way you do not suffer as much as or more than your neighbor from the same emotion. We are all the same in this regard.

Once a client told me, "I don't believe people suffer in the same way from emotions. For example, say that you and I are in the same situation, a dark deserted parking lot. You, a well-trained martial artist with a black belt, will not experience and suffer from fear as I do. I am not trained in any self-defense. I will suffer more than you do. You will not be afraid at all." And I answered honestly, "Of course I will experience fear, only a fool would not be afraid. Even a seasoned soldier will experience fear—it saves lives. Even James Bond will experience fear. But I use the energy of it properly. I will accept and use the energy of fear to be alert, to be cautious, to be quick with my decisions. And I will suffer from fear. My suffering might be shorter than yours, but it isn't less."

8.3 Step Three

The next step sounds very counterintuitive. Here you must accept and take in for processing the toxic emotions of others.

What? Wait! Don't you have enough to deal with? You have your own emotions! Now this!?

Calm down, my friend. Consider it a vaccination. It is typically easier to help others than to help oneself. Thus, it is easier for your body to accept someone else's emotion than to deal with your own. All will be well. This has been done for hundreds of years. You cannot argue with hundreds of years of research and development.

By taking in someone else's emotions, you are teaching your body to process emotions similar to your own. And don't forget to practice compassion. Compassion is a very important part of this transformation. It does magic.

And remember not to judge yourself or others for experiencing emotions. You experience emotions not because you are evil or good but because you are human. People don't become weak because of emotions. Brave soldiers are entitled to feel fear. It does not make them cowards.

You will not punish yourself or others for emotion. Face it: you cannot help it. Each emotion is the reaction of the "immune system" of your soul to the situation you are facing. Do you punish yourself for having a fever during the flu? No. The idea of it is absurd.

You will be patient with yourself and others. It takes time to learn and time to heal. You cannot console a widow and ask every five minutes, "Are you done?" You can't expect her to stop crying the moment you express condolences. It takes at least a year to process grief.

And you will not expect any changes or results from yourself or others. You cannot change others. You have no control over others. And you cannot expect any immediate change from yourself, because it takes time to change. It takes time to heal. It takes time to learn the lesson. It takes time to gain wisdom and build optimistic mind. For some: a week. For others: years.

Now let's start the meditation. You can download pre-recorded guided meditations from https://lando-medical-reiki-academy.thinkific.com/.

Preparation:

Let's start the meditation with a deep breath.

Become aware of your body.

Become aware of your feet.

Become aware of your legs.

Become aware of your torso.

Become aware of your hands.

Become aware of your arms.

Become aware of your shoulders.

Become aware of your neck.

Become aware of your head.

Become aware of your breath.

Step one: Acceptance

Become aware of the emotional discomfort (or you can use the name of the emotion you are working on).

With each breath accept the emotional discomfort gently, patiently, and lovingly, without judgment, without punishment, without expecting any change or result. Continue for 5-10 minutes or until you feel the release.

Step two: Awareness

Become aware that every single person in the world experiences similar emotional discomfort. And everyone suffers from this emotional discomfort. No one suffers more nor less. As we are all humans and we all have the same DNA, we all suffer the same from the same emotional discomfort.

Step three: Learning

With each breath take in everyone els'se emotional discomfort gently, patiently, and lovingly, without judgment, without punishment, and without expecting any change or result. And breathe out unconditional love towards all these people and yourself. Continue for 5-10 minutes or until you feel the release.

Finishing:

Become aware of your body.

Become aware of your head.

Become aware of your neck.

Become aware of your shoulders.

Become aware of your arms.

Become aware of your hands.

Become aware of your torso.

Become aware of your legs.

Become aware of your feet.

Take a deep breath and end the meditation.

9

WEEKLY PLAN

It is important to get yourself a nice planner made from good quality paper and a nice pen. You should use objects that mean something to you and that you bought for any sensible reason other than low price. This is a treat for yourself. Get a fancy leather-bound planner or a simple one. Get an expensive fountain pen from a famous maker with a solid gold tip or an ordinary one from the grocery store. It does not matter. What matters is that you cherish it. These will be your friends for a long time. Writing with your own hand (as opposed to using a keyboard and computer) creates a different connection between you and what you express on paper. Most famous writers still prefer old-fashioned paper and a pen. I love to write with a fountain pen—it really makes my creativity flow.

Each week read a chapter on one of the emotions. Do not rush to the next chapter. Keep working with each emotion for the recommended week even if you feel you don't have any problems processing it. You might be surprised. Practice makes perfect.

Create an action plan based on suggestions for the week. Your week might not start on Monday. In some places on this planet it starts on Sunday, in others on Friday. There are no set rules. It is your week, do whatever you want with it. I suggest if you start reading the chapter about emotion on Wednesday, start the next emotion on the following Wednesday. There is no better time than now to start training your optimistic mind.

For example, you are reading about anxiety. For each day of your week, allocate time for meditation. Don't allow anyone or anything to force you to change your plan. This is your life. This is your day, and you must start it right. No more pointless sacrifices.

Be thoughtful. Be deliberate. Be present. Good luck.

10

NURTURING OPTIMISTIC MIND

Once I was watching a very uplifting romantic movie with a girlfriend who was going through bad times. She was very depressed, and to cheer her up, I took her out. The love story was complicated, but it all ended well at the end—or so I thought. She began to cry. I got very worried and started asking if she was ok and why was she crying. Between sobs she wailed, "He ditched her!" The reply left me speechless because that was not what had happened. At least not according to the movie I just watched. I tried to argue with her, but it was useless. At that time, I knew nothing about optimistic and pessimistic minds and thought that all the sorrows of the soul could be fixed with an ice cream. It worked, she stopped sobbing, and we spent a few happy hours together. Unfortunately, neither ice cream nor my cheerful company could cure her pessimistic mind and the next day we were on the phone again. She was crying her heart out, and I was listening to her tragic life story.

At the time I could not figure out why she just didn't move forward and find a more considerate boyfriend. I did not understand it was her pessimistic mind that was pushing her back together with the person who abused her, neglected her, and made her feel miserable.

You are about to embark on amazing and difficult journey full of unexpected discoveries. Pessimistic mind is devious. Take your time and don't rush. Rome was not built in a day. All you have to lose is your pessimistic mind.

10.1 Eye Movement and Stress

Energy goes where our eyes go. Sudden unfortunate changes in your life increase Vata. When you are scared, anxious, or under stress, your eyes rapidly jump from one object to another. It steers energy and makes you even more Vata, creating a vicious cycle of stress and anxiety. Increased Vata reduces your ability to concentrate and make sensible and logical decisions.

Remember one thing: you are always in control. Don't let your monkey brain keep jumping and screaming every time someone cuts you off on the road. Train yourself to do the following while under stress:

1. Take control of your eyes.
2. Focus on one point.
3. Hold your gaze.
4. Take a few deep breaths.
5. When you feel you are calming down, keep the gaze steady and start thinking about solutions.

Be prepared to fail. And most importantly, don't be afraid to fail. Life is not a test—it is a journey. Every single skill you learn in this life requires hard work. No one becomes a champion without strenuous, regular training. When you fail, you learn and gain wisdom. This is how optimistic minds are built. Keep trying. You might not become an expert in meditation or enlightened, but you WILL learn practical, useful tools that will help you take control of your life and become a more comfortable and happier person. Can you imagine waking up in the morning flooded with the joy of being alive and well? That is your optimistic mind. You are welcome!

11

VATA: DISORIENTING EMOTIONS

This chapter describes Vata destabilizing emotions. Unbalanced Vata creates too much movement. It shortens time and makes us rush. It creates too much unnecessary stress. It forces us to make irrational decisions in haste. The best way to balance Vata is with meditation.

Let's do an experiment:

- Stand up.
- Put one hand over your chest.
- Put the other hand over your abdomen.
- Breathe your normal way and observe which hand moves more:
    - If your chest hand moves more, you breathe only with the upper portion of your lungs, depriving your body of much-needed oxygen. This type of breathing amplifies any stress and anxiety you experience.
    - If your abdomen hand moves more, you have a relaxed breath. This type of breath will help your body deal with any stress. Try to expand your abdominal breathing even more and observe how it makes you feel.

The best way to deal with any stressful situation is to take a deep breath first.

It is important to breathe deeply, extending the breath into your abdomen. Try not to breath with just the upper portion of your lungs.

Open your Book Companion and watch the video on how to do this breathing practice:

https://lando-medical-reiki-academy.thinkific.com/

Meditation is the practice of controlling your monkey brain. Did I just call you a monkey? Not at all. I called your brain "monkey brain." Why? Because your brain cannot sit still. It switches attention from one thing to another. It does not want to concentrate, to be still. It is addicted to entertainment, to constant noise, to distraction. It jumps from one thing to another like a monkey from one branch to another. It has no order. It creates chaos. It makes you stressed and robs you of valuable time. Monkey brain creates pessimistic mind. To relax, to make sensible decisions, you must learn to control your monkey brain first. Don't let your brain control you.

There is a simple exercise you can do to learn to control your monkey brain and start training your optimistic mind.

11.1 Monkey Brain Meditation

You can download a recording of this guided meditation from How to Train Optimistic Mind Book Companion at: https://lando-medical-reiki-academy.thinkific.com/

Preparation:

Let's start the meditation with a deep breath.

Become aware of your body.

Become aware of your feet.

Become aware of your legs.

Become aware of your torso.

Become aware of your hands.

Become aware of your arms.

Become aware of your shoulders.

Become aware of your neck.

Become aware of your head.

Become aware of your breath.

- Breathe in your normal way.
- Observe your breath. Pay attention to how it moves into your nose. How it expands your lungs. Note the pause between the inhalation and exhalation. Observe how your lungs contract to expel the air.
- Continue in this fashion for five minutes. Try not think any thoughts. If you wander away from observing your breath, gently remind yourself about what you are doing and return to meditation. Don't judge or punish yourself for wandering away.
- Now let's slow the breath. On the count of eight, breathe in, pause on the count of eight, exhale on the count of eight, pause on the count of eight. If slowing your breath in this way is difficult, try to start with a count of five. Gradually increase the count every week. Be gentle with yourself.
- Continue in this fashion for five minutes. Try not to think any thoughts. If you wander away from observing your breath, compassionately remind yourself what you are doing and return to meditation.
- Return to your normal breathing.

Finishing:

Become aware of your body.

Become aware of your head.

Become aware of your neck.

Become aware of your shoulders.

Become aware of your arms.

Become aware of your hands.

Become aware of your torso.

Become aware of your legs.

Become aware of your feet.

Take a deep breath and end the meditation.

Do this meditation every day. Be careful—you might become addicted!

Now let's talk about Vata emotions.

Imbalanced Vata creates anxiety, confusion, fear, insecurity, loneliness, and stress. Balanced Vata fosters creativity, focus, joy, ingenuity, flexibility, and playfulness.

11.2　Week 1: Anxiety

Pessimistic mind is an anxious mind, always fretting over small things. Optimistic mind is alert and ready to accept new information and act accordingly. You can see it when you observe a karate match. An experienced, well-balanced practitioner of martial arts never moves or blocks unless it is necessary. Unbalanced martial artists usually jump too much, block too hard, and reach too far, making themselves easy targets.

We experience anxiety when the situation around us is uncertain. Anxiety gives us the energy to be alert, to observe the smallest changes in our environment, to process all incoming information, and to choose the most effective response.

When you block anxiety, you create a dead end. We all admire athletes, actors, and speakers. We assume these people are gods with no human emotions to hinder their performance. But everyone experiences anxiety before a test or important game or performance. You are not alone. Anxiety does not make you weak. Anxiety, when accepted and not blocked, helps us to perform better.

As you meditate with anxiety, explore your sensations. When you take in the anxiety with each breath, do it slowly. Don't rush. Savor it as you would an expensive and rare dish prepared by a five-star Michelin chef. How does it taste, how does it feel, how does it smell? Is it thick or thin? What is the color of anxiety? Explore. Be curious. Let it float effortlessly into your body, like the fragrance of your favorite flower. It is just an emotion; it is just an energy (Prana in Ayurveda). You can control it. You can control how to use it. Be grateful you experience anxiety. It has kept human beings alive for millions of years. It would have been dangerous for our ancestors not to experience anxiety, because the saber-toothed tiger was always vigilant, and humans are quite delicious!

Let the anxiety float towards your heart. According to Ayurveda the pericardium is where the transformation happens. Trust your body to transform anxiety into compassion and love. Your body was designed this way. It is like breathing. You take in the air. It moves into your lungs, which know what to do with it. Your lungs require no supervision or encouragement. They take in oxygen, send it into the bloodstream, remove carbon dioxide from the blood, expel carbon dioxide. Likewise, your pericardium knows what to do with emotions. Let it do its magic.

Think about all humans. We are in the middle of a pandemic and war and famine are always present somewhere. How many people do you think are experiencing anxiety at this moment? You are just one of many. Just now I experienced a pinch of anxiety because I'm not sure if I'm explaining this to you clearly. It is easier to explain to a client. I can ask a question: does this make any sense to you? In the book I cannot fine-tune my explanation to each reader. It is written, printed, done. I am anxious, I am suffering, and I suffer the same way you do.

Let's breathe in someone else's anxiety. Let us explore it. Does it feel the same? The color? The smell? The shape? Gently and lovingly let it float to your heart and let your heart transform anxiety into love and compassion. Breathe out love and compassion. Keep meditating. Practice makes perfect.

When you master anxiety, it becomes a useful tool and strengthens optimistic mind. It helps you to stay alert, to evaluate rapidly changing situations. When you block anxiety, you become unfocused, you reinforce your pessimistic mind. It becomes difficult to live in the present moment. And if you cannot live here and now, you don't live. You cannot enjoy life, because life is here and now. The past is gone, and the future is not here. But you often unnecessarily worry about the past and the future. You cannot live in the past. It is already gone. As I am typing and you are reading, the present moment slips away into the past. It is gone. You are not there anymore, and you cannot go back even if you reread what I just typed. The future is not here yet. Why feel anxiety about something that does not exist? Optimistic mind lives only in the present moment.

You might want to try another useful practice. When you experience a lot or a little anxiety, take a deep breath and in the pause between the inhalation and exhalation acknowledge: "I am safe and alive here and now." For example, as you are reading this, nothing threatens you. Past threats are gone. So far you have survived all the calamities of your turbulent life. Good job! High five! New disasters are lurking in the future, but they are not real. They might happen or they might not. Why worry? At this moment you are reading (or listening to) my book, and all is well. This is the attitude of the optimistic mind. If you feel anxiety, put down this book. Don't worry, it will still be here, patiently waiting for you when you are done. Take a few deep highly enjoyable breaths and with each breath acknowledge: "I am safe and alive here and now."

The "I am safe and alive here and now" meditation is also available for you as a free download from How to Train Optimistic Mind Book Companion.

Plan for the week:
Get your paper calendar and block 10-20 minutes for daily meditation in the morning for the next 7 days.

Block 10 minutes in the evening for contemplation.

Download the "Toxic Emotions: Anxiety" meditation.

Day 1–3:

> Use your downloaded guided meditation to learn how to accept and use anxiety—5–10 minutes.

Day 4–7:

> Meditate with anxiety on your own without listening to the guided meditation—10–20 minutes.

From your library, try another meditation with the similar emotions of nervousness or stress and see which one works best for you.

Use your evening contemplation time to pay attention to how your reaction to situations that make you anxious, nervous, or stressed changes. If you experience a situation during the day that makes you anxious, do a short one-minute meditation with it. Acknowledge your reaction again and see if it changes.

Write about the situation in your planner and rate your emotion from zero to ten, where zero means anxiety does not cause any discomfort and ten means you have to go to the hospital because of a panic attack about tomorrow's sunrise.

11.3 Week 2: Doubt

Pessimistic mind always misses opportunities, always doubts itself, seldom trusts others.

Optimistic mind always sees the opportunities, always wants to try new things, is always ready to learn new things, always trusts others.

We all experience doubts. When you block this emotion, you cannot commit, make a final decision, or even follow up on your own choices.

Cats, for example, habitually have problems processing doubts. That's why they have nine lives. They can never decide "in" or "out" when St. Peter opens the gates of Heaven.

The energy of a doubt must be used to reconsider. Most likely new information is coming our way and must be studied. Doubt is the energy of contemplation and observation. It is very useful for cool-headed decisions.

You might think every time you make a choice you open yourself to new possibilities or new disasters. It is the worst assumption you can make. You don't open yourself to new possibilities OR new disasters. You open yourself to new possibilities AND new disasters. Life is never just a series of breathtaking successes. Life is never a series of devastating disasters. If you don't believe me, read the biography of Steve Jobs. Optimistic mind sees the possibilities and accepts disasters as opportunities to learn and gain wisdom. Pessimistic mind still broods over the choice it made during the first ice cream shop visit at the age of two.

Only in fairy tales do the "prince and princess live happily ever after." In real life they argue about spending at the mall and gambling and have heated discussions about inexpensive gifts to distant relations.

They refuse to talk to each other for years and move to different castles because they have a fleeting disagreement on whose turn it is to change a diaper. On a night of heavy drinking to celebrate their twentieth wedding anniversary the prince might reveal that he has deep regrets about choosing to explore the countryside looking for opportunities for heroic deeds, instead of spending a boring year in Europe as his boarding school graduation gift. He might even reveal, before he falls unconscious to his throne after finishing a bottle of 100-year-old brandy in one long skilled gulp, that young inexperienced men should never kiss sleeping strangers: "Let the sleeping viper and all her relatives sleep."

But it was his choice. Despite all the doubts, was it a total disaster? No, by marrying Sleeping Beauty, he doubled his possessions, had three adorable bright children, and brought political stability to his wife's kingdom. It was not all bad. Besides, if it had not been him, eventually someone else would find her and decide to kiss her red lips. Also, how many prudent, sensible young princes found her and chose not to kiss a stranger in a glass coffin for reasons of hygiene?

When meditating about doubts, be playful. Don't take any of your decisions too seriously. Even the best of us make wrong choices. So what? Mistakes become experiences. Experiences become lessons. Lessons become wisdom, and wisdom carries you to your dreams. Life is not a test, it is a journey. Often you might find yourself at a crossroad. For the optimistic mind it is thrilling. How will my life change if I turn left, or right, or go straight?

The energy of doubt helps to measure risks vs. rewards. Enjoy this energy, take your time, investigate, move forward. But be optimistic— it feels better, and you will learn one more lesson if you fail the first time. Optimistic mind uses the energy of doubt to gain wisdom.

Plan for the week:

Get your paper calendar and block 10–20 minutes for daily meditation in the morning for the next 7 days.

Block 10 minutes in the evening for a decision-making exercise.

Download the "Toxic Emotions: Doubt" meditation.

Day 1–3:

> Use your downloaded guided meditation to learn how to accept and use doubt—5–10 minutes.

Day 4–7:

> Meditate with doubt on your own without listening to the guided meditation—10–20 minutes.

Every evening use your decision-making time to review any daily decisions that have made you uneasy. Try to accept the energy of doubt to calm yourself; review the facts; and accept, decline, or change the decisions you have made. Write all your thoughts into your planner.

Rate your doubt from zero to ten, where zero means you are fine experiencing doubts and ten means you must call your mother to make a decision about your ice cream flavor.

11.4 Week 3: Fear

Pessimistic mind is always afraid of the outcome, always suspicious of people who look or act differently or have different world views, always dramatic.

Optimistic mind is always alert, always ready to adapt to the changing situation, always composed.

The emotion of fear carries the most useful energy for our survival. The body uses this energy in case of immediate danger. It fuels our reactions, mind, and muscles for split-second decisions.

"Paralyzed with fear" means that a person who experiences fear blocks it, and the body lacks necessary energies to deal with a dangerous situation. The body composes itself for a "war mode" and is ready to spring into action, but there is no electricity to fuel the engine.

A person who does not block the energy of fear is "locked and loaded." Their body utilizes the energy and is prepared to deal with any eventuality.

Remember, when you experience any emotion, you experience it the same way everyone else does. Unpleasant emotions are unpleasant to experience, whether you are a seasoned Navy SEAL or an elderly lady.

Let me tell you a story. In the middle of the night two people in two different cities are walking through a dark deserted parking lot next to a cemetery towards their cars. One is Jack, an experienced special forces major who just returned from one of his black ops. The second person is you. It is quiet and a little creepy. Suddenly both of you hear heavy steps behind you. Did you just jump? Sorry, I did not mean to scare you. It is just a story I wrote to make a point. Just step away from your own fear (take a deep breath if you need to) and tell me honestly: do you think Jack was scared, too? Why not? Jack is also a human. Not to mention Jack has more reasons to be scared than you. He might be a target of revenge. Remember, he just got back from a dangerous mission. Of course, you might be the target of a serial killer. Or a zombie. It is midnight and you are standing next to a cemetery after all ....

Let's agree that both of you have a healthy dose of fear of the unknown, and ungodly amounts of adrenalin are pumping through your veins. Jack, a well-trained soldier, knows how to use his fears. He takes a deep quiet breath, embraces his fears, and turns around to face his opponent. His body is pumped up with the energy of fear and adrenalin and is ready to react to whatever comes his way. And he gets a bear hug from his brother. Jack returns the hug and swears a lot to discharge the extra energy of fear and adrenalin. All is well. I am sorry if you are disappointed. But this is a self-help book, not a Tom Clancy novel. There are no fights to the last breath in my book.

But what about you? How is your zombie attack progressing? Well, maybe not a zombie, just a serial killer. You don't know yet. You have two choices. You can accept your fear and use its energy to turn around and face this terrible person only to discover an elderly lost gentlemen in white socks but no shoes. He does not remember his name and is very scared. Time to call the police and report that you found a lost Alzheimers patient. Good job.

But you also had a second choice: be paralyzed with fear by blocking it. The lost gentlemen's appearance in your peripheral vision might have cost you a heart attack, as he looks properly disheveled and suspicious.

You see? Fear does not make you a coward. It is your choices. And as it is your choice, who is now at the steering wheel? Yes! You!

Plan for the week:

Get your paper calendar and block 10–20 minutes for daily meditation in the morning for the next 7 days.

Block 10 minutes in the evening for a contemplation session.

Download the "Toxic Emotions: Fear" meditation.

Day 1–3:

> Use your downloaded guided meditation to learn how to accept and use fear— 5–10 minutes.

Day 4–7:

> Meditate with fear on your own without listening to the guided meditation—10–20 minutes.

Use your evening contemplation time to pay attention to how your reaction changes to scary situations. If you experience a scary situation during the day, do a short one-minute meditation with it. Acknowledge your reaction again and see if it changes.

Write about the situation in your planner and rate your emotion from zero to ten, where zero means you face an army of invading ugly aliens with cool determination because you know that the main character never dies in an American movie. Ten means when you see a spider you pray for deliverance and ultimately faint.

11.5 Week 4: Insecurity

Pessimistic mind is always afraid of being perceived as weak or different, is always afraid of expressing an opinion, and always tries to please.

Optimistic mind always has great confidence in its own abilities and skills, always recognizes its weak points and works on self-improvement, and is never afraid to express an opinion nor to be unique.

The feeling of insecurity causes a lot of unnecessary stress. Instead of allowing it to make you feel bad about yourself and about life in general, you should use the energy of insecurity to make adjustments and become more comfortable with yourself and open to new possibilities. You are still learning. It takes time and mistakes to learn.

You cannot learn without making mistakes. Does a mistake make you feel insecure? Good—use that energy to adjust and improve. I, for example, love yellow. To my disappointment, I have always looked horrible in yellow. It took me half of my life to figure out that lemon yellow is my color and orange yellow makes me look dead. Live and learn.

The great queen of fashion Chanel gave immortal advice that many women still follow with great success: after you dress up, look in the mirror before going out and remove one item of jewelry. Alexander

McQueen, on the other hand, might have given you different advice: look in the mirror before going out and add as much jewelry as you are already wearing.

It does not matter which fashion advice you follow. The important thing is how it makes you feel. Guess what: both royalties of the fashion world were using the emotion of insecurity to adjust their appearance and look absolutely fabulous. So can you. In truth, you already look absolutely fabulous without jewelry, the latest fashion trends, or the newest car. But if any of these things make you feel wonderful, why not go for it?

When you block the energy of insecurity, it is difficult to change, break old habits, end fruitless relationships, or quit an unsatisfying job.

When you learn to accept the energy of insecurity, you flow. This energy fuels creativity. You want to blend in? Use your creativity. Spies are very good at it. They can blend in anywhere. They can change their look from an old lady to a young punk or a drunkard in a matter of seconds, when in reality they might resemble your very ordinary boring uncle.

You want to stand out? Accept the energy of insecurity to keep your creativity flowing and put together the most outrageously elegant outfit that proclaims, "It is ME."

Feeling insecure about your job? Use this energy to get additional training and find a better one.

Feeling insecure in your relationship? You are right. Stop asking your friends if you look good together. You don't need a relationship dependent on outside confirmation of its quality. Move on. Use the energy of insecurity to get out of it and find your true soulmate.

Even great heroes experience insecurity, and it does not make them less heroic or less interesting. On the contrary, they look even more heroic as we watch them overcome their insecurities. In that galaxy far, far away, legendary Jedi Master and defeater of the evil emperor Luke Skywalker felt so much insecurity about his Jedi superpowers that the first time he tried to blow up the Death Star, he missed. Only by accepting the energy of insecurity was he able to connect to the Force and free the galaxy. As you might have noticed, even this extraordinary victory did not resolve his feelings of insecurity and he almost managed to lose his starship in a swamp. If not for his teacher Yoda, there would have been no more movies. Luke would have been trapped on Dagobah for the rest of his life. When Luke blocked the energies of insecurity, he lost faith in his own abilities to use the Force (despite all the previous events and everyone's encouragement). "I can't believe it," Luke said, when Yoda rescued his starship from the swamp. "That's why you fail," answered his teacher.

If you don't learn to accept the energy of insecurity, you will fail, too. But when you look at your defeats not as a final judgment of your abilities but as great lessons, you will grow and become a stronger person. So, please, do yourself a favor: stop letting your pessimistic mind mumble from dawn to dusk about how bad, stupid, unworthy, ugly, and clumsy you are. You are not. Taming the pessimistic mind might sound impossible. Be patient; it may take longer than you think.

The unprocessed energy of insecurity also leads to racism, discrimination, and bullying. People who accept and use the energy of insecurity do not perceive others as a threat and do not need to marginalize anyone. Optimistic mind does not need to judge others to feel better about itself.

Plan for the week:
Starting this week and moving forward, first thing in the morning when you look at yourself in the mirror:

- Look yourself in the eyes.
- Smile.
- Say: I love you.

Get your paper calendar and block 10–20 minutes for daily meditation.

Block 10 minutes in the evening for contemplation of your insecurities.

Download the "Toxic Emotions: Insecurity" meditation.

Day 1–3:

> Use your downloaded guided meditation to learn how to accept and use insecurity—5–10 minutes.

Day 4–7:

> Meditate with insecurity on your own without listening to the guided meditation—10–20 minutes.

Use your evening contemplation time to pay attention to how you felt during the day. If you are insecure about something, do a short one-minute meditation with it. Acknowledge your reaction again and see if it changes. Write about the situation in your planner and rate your insecurity from zero to ten, where zero means you are so confident you make a presentation to potential investors without any notes or preparations because your CEO is stuck somewhere in the Pacific Ocean after the only solar station on his private island exploded. And ten means you cannot go to the pharmacy to get medicine because you are not sure if your bank card is attractive enough to be used in public.

11.6 Week 5: Loneliness

Pessimistic mind is always afraid to be alone or left behind, always feels unloved, always worries that others have more fun at parties.

Optimistic mind does not need a crowd to feel good, does not need others to feel happy, is always independent and comfortable in a crowd or alone at home with a book.

Loneliness is a good energy for meditation, contemplation, and planning. It is the energy of silence. In our noisy world, when was the last time you enjoyed complete silence? Music in the stores, music on your phone, a steady stream of text messages and notifications.... Pessimistic mind needs these noises to feel important, needs notifications to feel included and happy. Optimistic mind does not need noise to feel happy. It does not need to be included.

Turn off everything. Think about you. What do you really want? Think about your creative projects. What do you want to start first? Think about your relationships. What do you want to improve? Think about the silence. It is a luxury. Enjoy it. Give your mind a rest.

Spend a few days a month alone with nature. I mean totally alone. Don't bring any friends or your phone with you.

What are the benefits of being alone in the natural environment? Too many to count. As research in Japan, Finland, and the United States shows, people who have a leisurely stroll in a forest or garden have lower stress levels, lower blood pressure, and a lower heart rate than those who walk for the same amount of time in an urban setting. Spending time in nature also makes you happier, relaxes your brain, increases creativity, and makes you kinder. Nature heals the pessimistic mind and nurtures the optimistic mind. Another study recently revealed that interaction with nature increases happiness and improves cognitive functions and mental health. [1]

Being alone is beneficial. Don't reach for your phone. Enjoy the silence. It is a luxury.

Plan for the week:

---

[1] *"Nurtured by nature", by Kirsten Weir, American Psychological Association, Vol. 51, No. 3, Page 50*

Get your paper calendar and block one minute of your time in the morning for the "smile in the mirror" ritual. You should make this a lifelong habit.

First thing in the morning when you look at yourself in the mirror:

- Look yourself in the eyes.
- Smile.
- Say: I love you.

Get your paper calendar and block 10-20 minutes for daily meditation in the morning for the next 7 days.

Block 10 minutes in the evening for contemplation

Block one weekend each month for your "alone with nature" time. Make this a lifelong habit.

Set the "do-not-disturb" feature on all your electronic devices from 6 p.m. to 10 a.m. If you cannot turn your phone off because you have a caretaking or similar obligation (for example, you must take care of your elderly parents), set your devices so that only the necessary people can bypass the blocking feature.

Download the "Toxic Emotions: Loneliness" meditation.

Day 1–3:

> Use your downloaded guided meditation to learn how to accept and use loneliness—5–10 minutes.

Day 4–7:

> Meditate with loneliness on your own without listening to the guided meditation—10–20 minutes.

Turn off your TV, radio, computer, and other electronic devices from 6 p.m. to 10 a.m. Don't worry, you and the world will be ok during this "absence." If you must, you can make exceptions on the weekends when you are not on your nature retreats. If you are deeply uncomfortable being disconnected from the world, I suggest you try it for at least a week when you work with the emotion of loneliness. Rate your stress level at the beginning and end of your week with no electronic devices in the evenings. Observe how your stress level has dropped.

Important: Don't ever leave your TV/radio running in the background. Move the TV/radio out of your bedroom and kitchen. It is more than white noise. TV/radio is not just for entertainment; it is used to sell things and to make you think in a certain way. If you let the TV/radio run in the background, your brain will still absorb its information and who knows how it will influence your decisions. Be in control.

Being lonely and making your own decisions requires bravery. Not many people are capable of it.

Spend one weekend every month alone with nature. If you are too busy, try for every other month. You don't have to spend a lot of money. Even turning off all your electronic devices, packing lunch, and spending the whole day in a local park or at the lake will do miracles.

Use your evening contemplation time to evaluate your feelings of loneliness throughout the day. If you feel very sad about loneliness, do a short one-minute meditation with it. Acknowledge your reaction again and see if it changes. It is important to understand that you are always lonely. It is your nature. It does not matter whether you have a family. It does not matter whether you have friends. Loneliness is not related to the number of people with whom you interact every day or the number of "likes" on your social media posts.

Every day of the week, describe why you feel lonely and sad in your planner and rate your loneliness from zero to ten, where zero means you never speak to a single person during the day, and you are not negatively affected. Ten means you must post the most flattering pictures of yourself on all social media repeatedly and garner numerous "likes" on your posts to feel part of a tribe.

12

PITTA: INFLAMMATORY EMOTIONS

Imbalanced pitta creates a lot of inflammation. It damages your digestive system and impairs the body's ability to absorb nutrients and fight diseases. So, it is vital that Pitta remain balanced.

Meditation and practicing transforming the emotions of anger, envy, impatience, and irritability into compassion and understanding are very important in cooling the Pitta.

12.1 Week 6: Anger

Pessimistic mind is always angry, raging, and needing a reason to fight. This gives Pitta a sense of importance and high position in society. Pessimistic mind never compromises, never considers others. Pessimistic mind is a bully and places the blame elsewhere.

Optimistic mind also sees the injustices of the world but instead of fighting, it tries to make changes to make the world a little better. Pessimistic mind insists on winning all the time. Optimistic mind looks for solutions and compromise.

Anger is the most powerful emotion. Anger does not make us bad. You are entitled to 360 degrees of all emotions. How can something that is your birthright make you bad? Your choices about how you use anger make you bad or good. You can and must use the energy of anger in a productive way. Anger is caused by injustice. You can turn the energy of anger into a force that changes the world into a kinder, more peaceful place.

Let's look at anger. When you view anger not as a negative force that you must suppress but rather as merely energy, you will see that it can be used in three ways:

- Annihilation: hurt the person who made you angry. This is not a very productive approach, as it leads to more anger and infinite escalation and suffering for both parties. For an example, look at the conflict between the Palestinians and Israel.

- Martyr: use it as a self-destructive force to hurt yourself. This is not a very good solution either, as it causes more suffering and grief among your friends and family.

- Compassion: use this energy in a productive way. You can turn the energy of anger into a force that changes the world into a kinder, more peaceful place. This is the the most difficult approach. But I never promised you that dealing with anger would be easy.

On a rainy afternoon, do you like to read a good book or watch a movie? Do you notice that nothing is given as a gift to the heroes we read about or watch? In each chapter, in each scene, they must fight for what they want. And these struggles are portrayed not only to make a book or a movie more interesting, but because these struggles reflect the nature of life. We all must work hard to obtain something authentic.

We are all accustomed to the easy way: fake it until you make it. This approach enforces pessimistic mind. And it only causes more suffering. Fake money is only valuable when you play Monopoly with friends. Just remember the real estate you now own is also fake.

Pretending not to be affected by something does not bring you any relief or resolution in a difficult situation. You act erratically. Endless sleepless nights lower your IQ and diminish your appearance so that in the morning, an unkempt stranger appears before you in the mirror. This is how pessimistic mind looks. When you master anger and nourish optimistic mind, you achieve something few people even dream about. You become a reliable, composed, caring person everyone wants to have as a friend. And do you know what is the best part? You would immensely enjoy your own company as well.

Sorry to repeat a cliché, but there is only one person who is hurt by your anger—you. Anger, that nasty untamed beast, secretly hides somewhere inside and rears its head in the most inconvenient moments of your life, making you look unstable. Just the mention of your ex can raise your blood pressure by 10 points.

The first step in taming anger is realizing that people are not bad. Mostly they go about their own business and feel sorry and ashamed when they hurt someone. You don't believe me? How do you feel when you accidently cut someone off on the road? Happy? Powerful? Terrified? Ashamed? Yes, I know. I feel the same. Ashamed mostly.

Let's do a little exercise. Imagine yourself driving your car, minding your own business, when suddenly someone cuts you off, almost hitting your front bumper. And they do it again to another car. And again! Where are the police when you need them?! Such people should be put in jail for a very long time and pay you a substantial amount of money to compensate for your pain and suffering. You feel as if only a month-long European trip can cure such devastating emotional injury.

Why does this scenario make you angry? Because you don't know this person's story. You think these sorts of people are just lurking on the highway, their only joy in life being to create havoc in the commute of good law-abiding citizens like yourself. Like vultures rising with the sun in search of breakfast, they come out of their hiding places just in time for the morning rush hour.

But it could also be your former co-worker whose mother just lost her battle with cancer. Your co-worker spent two sleepless nights at the hospice hoping for the impossible. The grief is too much for her. She must learn how to live with it. It takes time. Meanwhile, it lays heavy on her heart. It breaks her heart. She does not know where she is going. She is trying hard to be careful, but something is wrong with her vision. It might be tears. Yes, she should have called her friends to pick her up because she is no state to drive. But she also does not think clearly. Let her get home safely. Give her space.

Or it might be a young husband who just received a phone call that his wife's water broke, and he is rushing to get her to the hospital. No, I don't know why he did not call the ambulance. Maybe he did, but this heavy morning traffic makes it impossible for the ambulance to reach her in time. Were you so cool-headed when your first child was born?

Or it might be your friend who just found their significant other in a compromising situation with a stranger.

The point is that all the people around you on the road, in the grocery store, at the office, or on the phone have their own stories. As you have your own story. Some of these stories are sad, some are funny, and some are devastating. Some make you do things you never thought you, a very kind person, would ever do.

Optimistic mind uses the energy of anger to understand, to take care, to give space. One Buddhist proverb advises: "To understand everything is to forgive everything."

Anger has immense energy. Use it well. People change their behavior more willingly when approached with kindness. You are not an exception. I am sure you will change willingly if you stop nagging and talking down to yourself. When you learn how to use anger with compassion, you can change the world for the better, and what better place to start than with yourself? Are you angry at yourself for something you did or did not do? For making a mistake? When you recognize a mistake, it is a reason for great celebration, not self-flagellation. Because when you recognize something as a mistake, you have learned a great lesson. You will do better next time. There is no benefit in endless punishment of yourself for things you did last month, or last year, or in kindergarten. Life is not a test; life is a journey.

Does harboring anger against someone who did you wrong punish that person? I guarantee that they absolutely don't feel that anger. Can you feel their emotions? I don't think so.

Holding onto anger creates pessimistic mind. Forgiveness nourishes optimistic mind and makes you happier.

I once asked a client to let go of the anger she felt towards her philandering ex-husband. "But I would be letting him off the hook for what he did to me and our daughter," she replied. "Do you think you ever had him on the hook?" I asked.

Her ex-husband has his own lessons to learn. And until he learns them, he will always be cynical and unhappy and always wander from one relationship to another, going through life breaking hearts. Her anger and the anger of all other women do not make his life more miserable. He himself and his pessimistic mind make his life miserable. And when he finally learns his lesson, we should all rejoice, for he will stop bringing misery into the world.

But enough words. Let's practice conquering our anger. From now on when someone angers you, do the following exercise:

- Take a deep calming breath to take control of your pessimistic mind.

- Make up a story to tell yourself why this person might have behaved this way.

- Feel compassion towards this person for their predicament.

- Let the anger go.

This can be a dangerously effective exercise, as soon you might find yourself lacking situations that make you angry. Good, now you have more time to live. Optimistic mind wins!

Plan for the week:
First thing in the morning when you look at yourself in the mirror:

- Look yourself in the eyes.

- Smile.

- Say: I love you.

Get your paper calendar and block 10-20 minutes for daily meditation in the morning for the next 7 days.

Block 10 minutes in the evening for contemplation.

Download the "Toxic Emotions: Anger" meditation.

Day 1–3:

> Use your downloaded guided meditation to learn how to accept and use anger—5–10 minutes.

Day 4–7:

> Meditate with anger on your own without listening to the guided meditation—10–20 minutes.

Try to meditate with hatred, rage, and irritability (also available for download at Lando Medical Reiki Academy) and see which meditation works best for you.

Use your evening contemplation time to pay attention to how your response to other people's actions changes. If someone or something made you angry during the day, do a short one-minute meditation with this particular situation. Acknowledge your reaction again and see if it changes. Write about the situation in your planner. In addition, write a compassionate story about why you think this person acted the way they did. Rate your emotion from zero to ten, where zero means you experience a lot of compassion towards a slow-moving elderly lady crossing the street with her walker in front of your car at a red light when you are driving a friend with contractions to the hospital. Ten means you go ballistic every time you see someone who does not dress according to your high fashion standards.

12.2 Week 7: Envy

Pessimistic mind is always wounded by others' success stories, always finds the flaw, always criticizes, is always scheming to make others look bad to make up for its own miseries.

Optimistic mind learns from others' success. Optimistic mind is a great team player and always helps others achieve their goals. Optimistic mind is a great cheerleader.

We envy everyone and everything. Envy is an engine of progress. You would never have an opportunity to envy your co-worker's latest iPhone if someone somewhere in the forgotten darkness of history had not envied the new unusually shaped stone at the entrance of their neighbor's cave. Over time, that coveted stone led to great works of art, such as *Venus of Willendorf*, the *Taj Mahal*, *Mona Lisa*, and *Femme au chapeau rouge* (which sold in 2020 for $28 million).

Envy can be a good thing. Without it we would not have a wheel, a plow, a steam engine, or a space station. Envy can also be bad or just plain disastrous. Without it you would not have the fall of Rome, The

Wars of the Roses, or the Battle of Kohima. History would be very slow and uneventful without envy. You might wish for history to be boring for a change, but unfortunately it will not happen anytime soon.

Without envy, Shakespeare would not have written his great plays and sonnets. What would he have written about? *Richard III* would have been a dull sitcom with no plot to grab the attention of theater-loving Londoners.

In the heart of it all: life would be boring without envy.

Let us see how you can use envy productively. Nothing brings a point home like a personal story. Meet yours truly, humble author of this book, and my friend Valerie Remhoff, a talented Reiki Master and kinesiologist. We have known each other what seems like forever, we are in the same field, we have the same work experience, and we wrote a book together. We meet often for Reiki exchange or just for coffee. We like and respect each other. Do you think we never envy each other?

Once during one of our leisurely coffee breaks, Valerie mentioned that she had developed a new technique to calm imbalance based on Traditional Chinese Medicine principles. We both thought this particular problem could not be addressed in a simple way. And seemingly, she had figured it all out. Naturally, I am turning light green, my envy gradually deepening into a dark emerald.

At this point I had three choices. Choice number one: say nothing to her face, later publish a nasty compromising social media post to each and every platform accusing her of... of something, of anything; details do not matter. Imply she is not a good, loving Reiki Master but a nasty self-serving narcissist who likes to manipulate people.

Choice number two: start crying, go home, abruptly close my practice, stop answering phone calls, lock myself in the house, and cry myself into oblivion, because I am a worthless person who just pretends to be a good Reiki Master. Whom am I kidding? She is the only one.

In both cases pessimistic mind uses the energy of envy for destruction. But it can be used as a very productive force. If I don't want to ruin my friend or destroy my own career, what am I supposed to do with this envy? How am I to use it?

I took a deep breath, accepted the energy of envy, and used it to ask a simple question: How in the world did you do it? Valerie gladly explained while I listened, grateful for the fascinating lesson. I love when Valerie explains something. Her scientific mind creates beautiful logical concepts. After I returned home, I used the same energy of envy to look through my Ayurvedic books and research the problem.

Traditional Chinese Medicine and Ayurveda overlap but they are not identical. I might find similar principles to create a similar technique, or I might not. In the first case I would create something that would help my clients. In the second case I would just refer my clients who need this specific approach to Valerie. Everyone wins. Hurray to optimistic mind for seeing the opportunities.

There is a third option. During my research I might find information I forgot or overlooked when I first read that book. I might realize that I can create a unique technique to help one of my clients who has hit a snag in their progress. And guess what: I am certainly looking forward to telling Valerie about my discovery. Now she has the opportunity to turn green with envy, take a deep breath, and ask a question: How in the world...?

Envy is an amazing emotion. It is a powerful engine of progress, and it is used by optimistic mind for professional and spiritual growth.

Meanwhile, your next-door neighbor has mastered daily one-hour meditation. Feeling envious? Good, use this energy to increase your daily meditations to 30 minutes. There is no time like now.

Plan for the week:

First thing in the morning when you look at yourself in the mirror:

- Look yourself in the eyes.
- Smile.
- Say: I love you.

Get your paper calendar and block 30 minutes for daily meditation in the morning for the next 7 days.

Block 10 minutes in the evening for contemplation.

Download the "Toxic Emotions: Envy" meditation.

Day 1–3:

> Use your downloaded guided meditation to learn how to accept and use envy—5–10 minutes.

Day 4–7:

> Meditate with envy on your own without listening to guided meditation—30 minutes.

Use your evening contemplation time to pay attention to how your response to other people's success changes. If someone or something has made you so envious you were unable to breathe, do a short one-minute meditation with their success. Acknowledge your response again and see if it changes. Write about their success in your planner. Also describe how you can achieve the same, if not a better, solution to a problem of your own and why you think it will be a good idea to do so. Rate your emotion from zero to ten, where zero means you experienced joy over someone else's success because it proves a particular problem can be solved. Ten means you find so many serious faults in their book, movie, business, marriage, and children that you are infuriated about how they can fool the world with their rubbish.

12.3 Week 8: Egoism

Pessimistic mind can be a narcissist and see good things only in itself. Pessimistic mind always wants to be right. Pessimistic mind can also be a pleasing mind and go to great lengths to be loved and agreeable all the time.

Optimistic mind builds healthy boundaries. Optimistic mind can always assess its own abilities and readiness for tasks.

Egoism is a vital energy optimistic mind uses for self-preservation. When you block the energy of this emotion, it might equally nurture narcissism or force you to commit endless unnecessary sacrifices.

Egoism is the energy used when you establish healthy boundaries. Egoism helps you to develop a respectful, mutually beneficial relationship with a significant other, with a friend, or with a job. A healthy dose of egoism equally and respectfully exercised creates balance, happiness, and prosperity for both parties in any relationship. It creates a stable and long-lasting relationship where all parties are equal. Unprocessed egoism creates unstable relationships where everyone suffers from a destabilizing drama of dominance, submission, and guilt.

Once upon a time there lived Lord Bob with his wife. This mighty lord had a lot of emotional issues caused by the latest crusade and his difficult childhood with a tyrannical father who wanted him to become the greatest warrior. As a result, poor Lord Bob developed pessimistic mind. He was not a very good swordsman nor rider. And he was often kicked out of the army for falling off his horse or losing his sword in the heat of battle.

Instead of processing the energy of ego properly and declaring to the king and his own family that he was better at math and would be more useful to the king as a personal CPA than as a knight, he blocked ego and kept signing up for crusades, boasting about his supernatural skills with the sword.

At one of the feasts another knight, tired of his tall stories, called Lord Bob a fraud and challenged him to an honest sword fight. Which Lord Bob lost spectacularly. His pessimistic mind got so upset, he jumped in his carriage and left the feast without his wife. Her ladyship had to ask for a Lyft.

When she finally reached the castle in the middle of the night, her husband, fueled by the desire of pessimistic mind to always be right, accused her of never supporting or loving him as a good Christian wife should do. In front of their entire household, he announced an immediate divorce from her ladyship, tossed his shiny armor and dented sword into the carriage, and was gone. Despite their arranged marriage, his wife loved him and was inconsolable.

Two of her close girlfriends came to stay to give her comfort.

Lord Bob, after consulting a divorce lawyer and learning about an unpleasant provision in his prenuptial agreement that would leave his entire fortune to his wife in the case of abandonment and divorce, changed his mind. As Lord Bob's pessimistic mind wanted to be right all the time, Lord Bob had lost the ability to acknowledge his mistakes and, to avoid a humiliating apology, developed a cunning plan.

He returned home, accused the two girlfriends of scheming to break up his happy marriage, declared the divorce null and void as it was forced upon him, and promised to return home only if his wife banned the two conspiring girlfriends from his castle. Her ladyship gladly agreed, and they lived happily ever after—for three years, anyway, until he left and returned again, and then repeated the whole charade every three years just to keep his wife on her toes. All was well, but her ladyship was distressed by the peculiar fact that her two dearest girlfriends were always absent from their castles every time she tried to visit (sneaking away from her husband, of course, to do so).

Yes, you might call Lord Bob a manipulating bastard. But her ladyship also had the choice whether to stay in a melodramatic, unstable relationship or process her ego properly, nourish optimistic mind, set up boundaries, and kick screaming and scheming Lord Bob into the stinky moat with his shiny armor, dented sword, unprocessed ego, and pessimistic mind.

Once upon a time (in the past or in the future) you might have found, or find, yourself a willing participant in a melodramatic, unstable relationship. With experience you will start recognizing an invitation to this type of relationship before it begins. I hope you practice meditations enough to use ego energy to decline the invitation politely but firmly. And the next time your boss calls you at an ungodly hour with dramatic declarations of the demise of the company only you can save, preaching the beauty and goodness of overtime, you know what to do first thing in the morning: work on your resume.

Plan for the week:
First thing in the morning when you look at yourself in the mirror:

- Look yourself in the eyes.
- Smile.
- Say: I love you.

Get your paper calendar and block 30 minutes for daily meditation in the morning for the next 7 days.

Block 10 minutes in the evening for contemplation.

Download the "Toxic Emotions: Egoism" meditation.

Day 1–3:

> Use your downloaded guided meditation to learn how to accept and use egoism—5–10 minutes.

Day 4–7:

> Meditate with egoism on your own without listening to the guided meditation—10–20 minutes.

Use your evening contemplation time to review your interactions with other people during the day. Were these interactions stable or dramatic? If you notice you are not processing ego well and don't build good boundaries, do a short one-minute meditation with the emotion of ego. Acknowledge your response again and see if it changes. Describe instances where you had to use ego to build boundaries and balance relationships. In addition, describe situations where you fell into unstable dramatic relationships and, using the energy of ego, create ways to end or balance, if possible, these dramatic relationships. Rate your emotion from zero to ten, where zero means you easily walk away when you recognize that someone is trying to manipulate you into a dramatic relationship. Ten means you feel so guilty for breaking up your family, you petition a judge to lift a restraining order on your abusive spouse.

12.4 Week 9: Frustration

Pessimistic mind never learns and makes the same mistakes over and over. It gets angry at circumstances that do not magically align to accommodate its needs. Pessimistic mind never improves itself and never gains wisdom.

Optimistic mind always assesses the situation and always adjusts. It tries many approaches to accomplish whatever is necessary. Optimistic mind gains wisdom and experience.

Do you feel like banging your head on the wall every time the Internet slows down to a dial-up speed? You don't know what dial-up speed is? You are so young! First, it is an oxymoron. There was no speed with dial-up. You could click on a link, go out with friends, and return in a few hours to read the first half of the page while the second half of the page was still loading. Yes, my generation was very patient, and digital technology was very ancient, but don't write us off yet. Somehow, we managed to build a space station and send Rover to Mars. No, the generation before us sent man into space. They used paper and pen to do most of the calculations. Imagine that!

Back to your slow Internet. The emotion of frustration is very useful. But if you block it, you will keep banging your head on the wall. Unfortunately, it will not help you. Frustration might feel blinding, but if you process it properly, all will be well. Use the energy of frustration to evaluate your predicament, do a quick hardware check, and remove the sleeping cat from the router. You see, I told you all would be well. You are learning.

Next time use the energy of frustration to repeat the same steps and, if removing sleeping cat from the router doesn't help, call tech support. Keep utilizing the energy of frustration as you work through the conversation with a chatbot. When you feel blinding rage against it, use the energy of frustration to tell a compassionate story about artificial intelligence. Why do you think it acts like an idiot? It might not be designed properly, or maybe it accidentally accessed the wrong database. If there is still no solution, use the energy of frustration to calmly keep pressing zero until the bot gets frustrated with you and uses the energy of its frustration to connect you to a live person with an incomprehensible accent. Use the energy of frustration to politely ask to talk to someone who can understand your English. All will be well.

It is vital to process the energy of frustration. If your parents, for example, blocked it, you would not have made it to adulthood. The energy of frustration moves an innovation forward.

Frustration arises when something is not happening the way you assume it should happen. You must use this energy to evaluate the circumstances and your methods and design a new approach—or find yourself a better project.

Blocked energy of frustration makes you keep doing things that do not bring any results. Many businesses large and small failed because management did not process frustration properly and kept producing carriages; meanwhile, their clients switched to cars and bicycles. Many people block frustration and end up spending their entire lives in miserable relationships.

All the failings of the world are fueled by blocked frustration, which in turn contributes to wars, famine, stagnant legislation, bad laws, and abusive relationships.

Don't let frustration fool you. Use it to find a sensible solution. There is always a sensible solution.

Plan for the week:

First thing in the morning when you look at yourself in the mirror:

- Look yourself in the eyes.
- Smile.
- Say: I love you.

Get your paper calendar and block 30 minutes for daily meditation in the morning for the next 7 days.

Block 10 minutes in the evening for contemplation.

Day 1–3:

> Use your downloaded guided meditation to learn how to accept and use frustration—5–10 minutes.

Day 4–7:

> Meditate with frustration on your own without listening to the guided meditation—30 minutes.

Also try to meditate with impatience and see which meditation is best for you.

Use your evening contemplation time to review your interactions with people and companies during the day. Did you experience frustration? If you notice you are not using the energy of frustration to resolve the issues, do a short one-minute meditation with frustration. Acknowledge your reaction again and see if it changes. Describe situations where you got frustrated. Also describe the best solution to resolve the situation in the most productive way. Rate your emotion from zero to ten, where zero means you coolly, without raising your voice, explain to tech support on the phone for the hundredth time that you did not disconnect the computer from the power source just before Windows crashed (give yourself a pat on the shoulder for addressing them Sir or Miss). Ten means you bang your head on the wall when your three-month old puppy refuses to follow your command.

12.5 Week 10: Jealousy

Pessimistic mind is distrustful and possessive. Pessimistic mind is cynical. To feel secure, it wants everyone and everything for itself.

Optimistic mind is loving and kind. Optimistic mind gives space.

Jealousy is a powerful emotion that can be used to enhance your relationship or to destroy it. Everyone experiences jealousy. The difference between successful and failing marriages is the difference between processed and blocked jealousy.

Love requires a lot of work. It is entropic. You cannot just expect it to thrive without attention. You must work hard to preserve it. It is not a prize that can be won once. Love is a relationship and relationships fluctuate. Couples experience good days when both people are happy and full of energy. And couples experience bad days when both are tired and irritable. And couples experience mixed days.

When processed correctly the energy of jealousy gives you the fuel to go that extra mile. It gives you the drive to smile when you are upset, to cook dinner when you are tired, to hold hands when you want to be left alone, to buy flowers when you are too busy. Jealousy helps you to do all these little insignificant things that, when combined, create love.

When you process jealousy correctly, it helps you to understand that true love is free to love and true love is free to leave. And the words "until death do us part" are empty without significant effort by both parties fueled by the energy of jealousy.

Blocked jealousy destroys love, marriages, and friendship. It makes people lose their minds and commit murder.

Let's dissect Bizet's famous opera *Carmen*. Unprocessed jealousy plays the main part in this tragic story. In fact, it is probably the hero of the opera. It starts when beautiful Carmen, surrounded by an adoring crowd, gets upset at the officer Jose, who does not appreciate her charms. If Carmen would process the emotion of jealousy, she would not need validation of her beauty and status by getting the admiring attention of every man she meets. She would just choose one and settle down. Instead, her pessimistic mind runs wild and wants every single man for itself. Unfortunately for Carmen and everyone else, her pessimistic mind, confused by emotional blockages, sends ambiguous signals to Jose.

Poor Jose, influenced by the customs of his times, lost the ability to process jealousy a long time ago. He deserts his post in the army and becomes a plaything to Carmen.

Regrettably, Carmen's unprocessed jealousy not only makes her unable to fall in love; it also drives her thirst for conquest. She soon loses interest in "conquered" Jose and finds another more prestigious target: a famous toreador. Unprocessed jealousy drives Jose mad, and he kills Carmen.

If Carmen could have processed her own jealousy and transformed it into caring for Jose or someone else instead of nurturing her own insecurities and tormenting him, she would have lived and had ten adorable children.

If Jose had known how to process jealousy, he would have understood that Carmen was not a good match, and he would have remained with his regiment. Unfortunately for Carmen and Jose, psychoanalysis was years away, Sigmund Freud was not even born, and my book was not published yet!

Love is precious and fragile. Use jealousy to find love, to build love, and to preserve love. Pessimistic mind destroys relationships. Optimistic mind preserves and enhances relationships.

Plan for the week:
First thing in the morning when you look at yourself in the mirror:

- Look yourself in the eyes.
- Smile.
- Say: I love you.

Get your paper calendar and block 30 minutes for daily meditation in the morning for the next 7 days.

Block 10 minutes in the evening for contemplation.

Download the "Toxic Emotions: Jealousy" meditation.

Day 1–3:

> Use your downloaded guided meditation to learn how to accept and use jealousy—5–10 minutes.

Day 4–7:

> Meditate with jealousy on your own without listening to the guided meditation—30 minutes.

Use your evening contemplation time to review the feeling of jealousy. Did you feel any? How did you use it? Describe situations where you got jealous and how you used this energy. Do you think you can do better? Rate your emotion from zero to ten, where zero means you are amused by someone openly trying to set up a date with your spouse or partner with you standing nearby—you think it is hilarious! Ten means you pack your bags and leave when your significant other smiled while thanking the barista at the coffee shop.

12.6 Week 11: Judgment

Pessimistic mind judges everything and gives its unkind, unsolicited opinions. Pessimistic mind wants everyone to live up to its own impeccable standards. Pessimistic mind always judges and makes itself more miserable. The only way pessimistic mind can feel better is when it experiences the ecstasy of righteousness.

Optimistic mind is content with itself. It does not constantly judge others because it has better things to do. Optimistic mind makes decisions based on evaluation. Optimistic mind wants the world to be diverse. It is opened to new experiences.

Without judgment you would be unable to find safe food, choose a reliable partner, or dress suitably. It helps us to see who is trustworthy.

Without judgment you would be taking sewing classes when all you really want is to advance in your IT field.

Without judgment the world would slip into sometimes hilarious, sometimes tragic, chaos. The Olympics, the Oscars, and dancing competitions would be doomed.

Judgment is very handy and, I might say, solely responsible for the survival of our species. On the other hand, World War II might not even have started if the German chancellor, after coolheadedly evaluating his country's resources, decided that "liberating" Europe was not worth the trouble of losing ten million of his own countrymen. Many who fail to judge situations properly receive a Darwin Award— sometimes posthumously.

When you block the energy of judgment, things get even more interesting. Oh, the ecstasy of righteousness! If everyone would process the energy of judgment instead of blocking it and becoming enraged, Nationalism, Communism, Fascism, and McCarthyism would not exist for the lack of willing supporters. We would be deprived of the spectacle of virtuous crowds gathered in front of courthouses demanding the appropriate (according to current beliefs) verdict of guilty or innocent, even before the first witnesses are called. Many politicians would be forced to participate in meaningful legislation and do something authentic for their communities instead of boiling with fake indignation over a well-organized spontaneous rally. And poor king George III would not have lost an expensive shipment of tea, thirteen colonies, and a multitude of business opportunities in Louisiana, Florida, and Alaska.

When you process judgment, it enhances your life skills. The proper use of judgment helps you better understand the dynamics of relationships between you and other people. If you are dating, it will help you find the best match, recognize deceitful people, and screen out marauding buccaneers. When you don't process judgment, dating becomes a nightmare. The misuse of judgment starts with your online profile. You subtract pounds from your weight, years from your age, and add or remove inches from your height. You post the most flattering, professionally retouched picture of you from ten years ago. Unprocessed judgment makes you fret about what people will say or think about you. It moves your benchmark from "what is best for me" to "what my neighbors might say." To compensate for constant unhappiness, unprocessed judgment makes you look down on others. And for a fleeting moment, the ecstasy of righteousness makes you feel happy. But then your misery sinks in and the vicious cycle of going from feeling inferior to feeling superior through righteousness continues.

Saying "Who taught him how to drive?" makes you feel better about your own driving. "She looks fat" makes you feel good about your own failing efforts to lose weight. "She looks old" makes you forget about your own wrinkles and laugh lines.

No one might notice your constant grumpiness, but it takes an irreparable toll on your success and well-being. Not only does judgment take too much time from your creative processes; it also makes you unhappy and sick.

When the marma point Jatru (which means Preserver) is blocked by unprocessed judgment, it weakens your immune system; disrupts detoxification; makes you fatigued; and can trigger breathing problems, respiratory infections, and asthma. It can cause thyroid problems and goiter and shorten your life span.

You cannot stop judging and unblock the energy flow by sheer will. First, you must learn to stop judging yourself. Only then will you be able to stop judging others because you have no need for the drug of righteousness. You will feel good without it. And you will free up so much time for thinking about a new interesting project or starting a new business or family. You will also have more time to meet with friends and talk about something meaningful and substantial and stop complaining about the traffic. Traffic was bad for the ancient Romans and shows no signs of improvement. So, get used to it, unless you work for the Department of Transportation— then your obsession is understandable and can benefit the community.

Processed judgment promotes appropriate benchmarks. What seems more tenable: "What do the neighbors think?" or "What is best for me and my community?"

There is a Mirror of Erised in the first book of Harry Potter. It reveals to someone the person's deepest desires. Only someone who can process judgment correctly will see themselves as they truly are. What do you see in the Mirror of Erised? A thinner, younger, smarter you? But it is not you. You are here and now. You are full of possibilities, magic, and delight. Instead of judging yourself, instead of subjecting yourself to the illusory standards of filters, Photoshop, and fake perfectionism, you should proclaim your uniqueness and unconventional talents to the world. There is no one in the world like you.

Let the energy of judgment fuel your integrity and your path. Let it be a guide in the murky, confusing waters of everyday life. Let it free you from the fear of not being like everyone else, because each and every one of us is unique.

If Rafael, DaVinci, Picasso, and Van Gogh did not process judgment properly, they would still paint in the same safe way as others before them, and you would not have the Sistine Madonna. If J.K. Rowling were afraid of people's opinions and wrote only novels that she believed would sell well, we would be deprived of the delights of Harry Potter. And if Steve Jobs cared too much about the opinion of his board of directors, you would not have a little miracle in your pocket with more computing power than we used to send the first man into space.

And while we are on the subject of Rafael: If he had been such an obedient student and always hid his sense of humor so that he could be a "proper" artist, we would not have a delightful secret in the painting of the Sistine Madonna. And I would not have the pleasure of asking you to find the painting (a reproduction, or you could travel to Germany and look at the original) and count the fingers on the right hand of Saint Sixtus. Enjoy!

Plan for the week:

First thing in the morning when you look at yourself in the mirror:

- Look yourself in the eyes.
- Smile.
- Say: I love you.

Get your paper calendar and block 30 minutes for daily meditation in the morning for the next 7 days.

Block 10 minutes in the evening for contemplation.

Download the "Toxic Emotions: Judgment" meditation.

Day 1–3:

> Use your downloaded guided meditation to learn how to accept and use judgement—5-10 minutes.

Day 4–7:

> Meditate with judgment on your own without listening to guided meditation—30 minutes.

Use your evening contemplation time to review if you feel judgmental. Describe situations in which you were judging others unkindly and why. Rate your emotion from zero to ten, where zero means you calmly resist peer pressure to see the latest and greatest show on Netflix (in its fifteenth season) because you find more interesting things to do with your spare time. Ten means you cannot go to a restaurant by yourself because you are afraid a waitress will think you don't have a spouse.

12.7 Week 12: Pride

Pessimistic mind is a boasting mind. Pessimistic mind takes credit without doing anything. It feels too important to be bothered.

Pessimistic mind is unapproachable and dismissive. It is afraid to take responsibility. Pessimistic mind can also be too shy to acknowledge success.

Optimistic mind always evaluates progress. Optimistic mind accepts responsibility. It is always in control.

As you go through the day from one task to another, it is important to understand if your activities make your life and the lives of people around you better and to let the happiness of satisfaction propel you to the next task. Properly processed pride makes you feel better. It is a reward for a job well done. It fuels your next project.

When the emotion of pride is blocked, it might lead to the development of vanity or false piety. Either way, chaos can result. Because vanity makes people boast about the most mundane accomplishments to no end, they waste valuable time that could have been used to actually make the world better. And falsely pious people disturb the energy balance by not accepting gratitude and not permitting themselves to experience the joy of accomplishment to fuel the progress of their lives. The energy of pride not only helps you analyze your accomplishments; it also helps you accept rightfully earned praise and rewards.

Once upon a time somewhere in the Middle East lived a young mischievous Genie. He had a hard time processing pride and as a result, unbeknown to himself, was under the complete control of pessimistic mind. His ability to judge situations properly was impaired. Pessimistic minds are not all gloom and doom. Genie found great pleasure in the pranks he played on humans and boasted about his adventures and lucky escapes to other genies.

When Genie was working at the court of a sheikh, he played so many practical jokes on his master that the sheikh got very angry. He asked his vizier, a powerful magician, to fire Genie, but in a way that would not endanger their kingdom, already weakened by Genie's latest escapade causing it to rain live cats and dogs for two straight hours. The shrewd vizier invited Genie and a few close friends to a lavish dinner cooked by his famous French chef.

During the dinner Genie amused himself by turning tender lamb into spinach on guests' plates and by making apricots sprout long spider legs and flee into the vizier's harem, where much excitement ensued. The vizier clapped his hands in feigned delight. He then made a bet that Genie could not make himself fit into a small bottle. Little Genie knew that this particular bottle was a very old model without a safety latch on the inside. The moment Genie disappeared into the bottle, the vizier closed it and threw it into the sea. Upon this news the whole kingdom burst into celebration and rushed to adopt the rest of the cats and dogs from the overcrowded pet shelters.

For centuries Genie was floating in the ocean. Eventually he was found by a very pious person. Genie was so delighted he offered to fulfill three wishes for her. Unfortunately, this pious person never learned to process the emotion of pride. So, she refused to accept Genie's gift. It was a big loss for humanity, as her secret wishes were to open a pet shelter, have an unlimited flow of donations, and save the Middle East from a persistent mysterious epidemic of stray cats and dogs.

Plan for the week:
First thing in the morning when you look at yourself in the mirror:

- Look yourself in the eyes.
- Smile.
- Say: I love you.

Get your paper calendar and block 30 minutes for daily meditation in the morning for the next 7 days.

Block 10 minutes in the evening for contemplation.

Download the "Toxic Emotions: Pride" meditation.

Day 1–3:

> Use your downloaded guided meditation to learn how to accept and use pride—5-10 minutes.

Day 4–7:

> Meditate with pride on your own without listening to the guided meditation—30 minutes.

Use your evening contemplation time to pay attention to how you feel about your accomplishments for the day. Do you feel proud about your twelve-week meditation journey? You should. Many people would have quit by now and be parked in front of the TV. If you become aware of having refused to experience pride during the day, do a short one-minute meditation. Observe your response again and see if it has changed. Write about your accomplishments. Rate your pride from zero to ten, where zero means you experience innocent joy when you complete even the most trivial tasks. Ten means you still happily remind everyone that if not for you, your neighbor would have died from starvation five years ago when you picked up an apple that fell from her grocery bag.

13

KAPHA: STAGNANT EMOTIONS

As you remember, Kapha is a combination of water and earth. Kapha people are loving and compassionate. But when Kapha goes out of balance, it brings stagnation and boredom. In a balanced state, Kapha people are pillars of the Earth—reliable, determined, and loyal. In an unbalanced state, they are killjoys, pessimistic, ultra-conservative, and resistant to change.

13.1 Week 13: Attachment

Pessimistic mind clings to outdated rules and ideas. It is greedy and stubborn. Pessimistic mind is ultra-conservative. It does not like change. It is obsessed with insignificant details.

Optimistic mind knows its goal. It is reliable and constant. Optimistic mind is steady and trustworthy. It cannot be easily seduced by fame or bribes. Optimistic mind is faithful.

Attachment can be our best friend or our worst enemy. It all depends on you. Do you have a big goal? Then use the energy of attachment to strengthen the commitment and enthusiasm you feel about your goal. Do you "sweat the small stuff"? Use the energy of attachment to realize what is important.

I agree that it is easier said than done. Imagine that you are a pirate. Don't worry—I am not sending you on any dangerous and criminal mission. The pillaging and looting will have to wait! You are not just a pirate, you are the captain of a magnificent three-mast frigate, the fastest in the Atlantic Ocean. You and your crew got a little tired from all the overtime you had to put in to finish your latest project chasing rich Spanish ships (even your friend, a lawyer in Port Royal, does not work outlandish thirty-hour workweeks). So, you decide to take a little time off at an all-inclusive resort in Puerto Rico.

You goal is to have a little "me" time: sleep until midday, have a massage or two, do yoga, eat healthy. Your crew is delighted at the prospect of a hot shower and clean underwear. Everyone on board has developed an unquenched attachment to the idea of the well-deserved vacation at the all-inclusive resort and the opportunity to spend ill-gained fortune. You adjust your bearings, change course, and set full sail forward towards the Puerto Rican sunrise.

Meanwhile, you decide to clean the ship to arrive at the port in all her glory. As a proper Zen teacher is hard to find among pirates and all your knowledge about enlightenment and meditation comes from YouTube videos, you unintentionally block the energy of attachment. This blockage causes you to get unreasonably mad about the cleanliness of the ship. You demand to stop twice a day and send the crew into the shark-infested water to remove barnacles. And when you change course again to spend two fruitless hours chasing the whale that chipped off an ornamental piece near the back anchor, you have a mutiny on your hands. Your crew, still feeling a strong attachment to the all-inclusive vacation, hot showers, and clean underwear, use the energy of attachment the only way they know how. They take over the ship and drop you on a deserted island that no one has any knowledge of.

The good news is that now you can practice meditation and yoga all day long without any interruption.

Your crew, after it has processed the energy of attachment properly, navigates towards the port and now enjoys hot showers and clean underwear. Your only hope is that they will use their "me" time for quiet contemplation on the anger they experienced towards you, find the way to turn it into forgiveness and compassion, and feel enough remorse to return and find the island where they dropped you off.

If pirating is not your thing, maybe a dating example will prove more relevant. Let's say you want to get married and have a family. Your goal is to have a big wedding with a white dress, a huge cake, and a honeymoon at an all-inclusive adults-only resort in Puerto Rico.

If you keep your attachment focused on building a happy family, you will properly and easily use the energy of attachment to filter out all unsuitable potential spouses. There will be no sleepless nights and calls to the Psychic Network to find out why the love of your life did not text you back immediately after you sent a "kiss-kiss" emoji at 3 a.m. There might be no big wedding or even a honeymoon. But if you are focusing your attachment energy on the happy marriage, everything else is not that important.

You also have the option to focus on a big wedding and expensive honeymoon. You might run into slight problems, as the number of rich potential spouses are limited even with Bill Gates, Rihanna, and Jeff Bezos coming back on the market.

But if you stop processing attachment properly and instead of spending this energy on screening for a soulmate or a sugar daddy or mamma you get attached to everyone you meet online, in real life, and on the big screen, you are heading for a colossal emotional wreck. You will lose the ability to properly screen out inappropriate matches and to distinguish between reality and your fantasies.

Don't confuse attachment with love. These are two different things. Love is mutual. Attachment to unattainable love is unprocessed attachment.

I once had a client in his fifties who was still in love with his high school sweetheart. She was happily married with two children and knew nothing about the torch he was carrying for her. He obviously had a hard time processing attachment. It manifested not just in his secret unfulfilled love, but also in other aspects of his life. He was miserable. Nothing made him happy. I tried to teach him how to release attachment and start processing emotions properly. I wish I could tell you a story with a happy ending. But he did not want to let his "true big tragic" love go. He did not want another life. There was no happily ever after with two kids for him. It was his choice.

What is your choice? Is your choice to follow all the rules you learned in kindergarten? Is your choice to follow the footpath your parents or society pushed on you? Is your choice to follow the expectations of your friends? Is your choice to follow the fantasy that cannot be fulfilled because you don't have the predisposition for it? When you accept the energy of attachment, it helps you release unrealistic goals and find your own unique track. The sky is not the limit.

Plan for the week:

First thing in the morning when you look at yourself in the mirror:

- Look yourself in the eyes.
- Smile.
- Say: I love you.

Get your paper calendar and block 30 minutes for daily meditation in the morning for the next 7 days.

Block 10 minutes in the evening for contemplation.

Download the "Toxic Emotions: Attachment" meditation.

Day 1–3:

> Use your downloaded guided meditation to learn how to accept and use attachment — 5–10 minutes.

Day 4–7:

> Meditate with attachment on your own without listening to the guided meditation—30 minutes.

Use your evening contemplation time to pay attention to how you plan your day and how much time you spend on insignificant meaningless tasks. If you become aware of things you do just out of habit or because you cannot let senseless objectives go, do a short one-minute meditation with your attachment to these items, tasks, or people. Acknowledge your reaction again and see if it changes. Write about your attachments and why you think they are important. Rate your emotion from zero to ten, where zero means you keep your eyes on your big goal of making your life meaningful and productive and can tell the difference between tasks that will propel you forward and tasks that will hold you back. Ten means you cannot let go of the old socks you wore during the first date with your second ex.

13.2 Week 14: Lethargy

Pessimistic mind is always depressed. It is always lazy and too discouraged to start anything. Pessimistic mind drags itself through life. It is desperate, yet always gives up.

Optimistic mind embraces rest. Optimistic mind is always hopeful and well prepared for setbacks. Optimistic mind never gives up.

I might surprise you by telling you that lethargy is very healthy. You might object and argue that it prevents you from doing things you must do. Exactly! This is the point. Everyone needs a rest.

Ayurveda recognizes that Doshas affect not just humans, but the entire Universe. Periods of human life are divided into Vata periods, Pitta periods, and Kapha periods. Seasons are divided into Vata seasons, Pitta seasons, and Kapha seasons. The time of the day is also divided into Vata time, Pitta time, and Kapha time.

Vata periods are full of movement. Sometimes they are chaotic and destructive, but they can also be inspiring and revealing. Pitta periods are full of productive energy. And Kapha times are slow and restful.

During the day you experience two pairs of Vata, Pitta, and Kapha periods. The first Kapha period is in the morning, a slow time for building a foundation for a new day. It is followed up by a Pitta period, the best time to work. A Vata period follows, when you evaluate your day's work and plan for the next day. The second Kapha period starts in the evening and helps you to calm and get ready for bed. Then is another Pitta period during your sleep, when the body is using the energy of Pitta to repair and detoxify the body. Finally, there is another Vata period, when all the waste and toxins start moving out to be ready for elimination in the morning.

Just as your body needs periods of rest, repair, and elimination, so does your soul.

Western thought also supports this theory. Dr. Natalie Winters, my mentor and the recipient of the J.L. Moreno Lifetime Achievement Award and ASGPP Innovators Award, came up with a soul development theory. According to this theory, the soul must go through certain stages to continue proper development. The first stage is creativity. During this stage everything is getting done. You feel inspired and full of energy. Your soul is happy and very active. The second stage is stagnation. Stagnation is the periods of your life when you feel lethargic, unmotivated, lazy. Your soul is asleep. Nothing comes easy. It is followed by a third stage: accumulation. This is the period of awakening. Your soul wakes up and is ready to embrace the world in its beauty, learn new things, and be inspired. This period leads to the period of creativity, creativity leads to stagnation, and stagnation to accumulation. You see? Your soul must rest, too. Not just your body.

When you accept the energy of lethargy, your soul recharges and rests. The more you fight to stay "awake," the longer and more painful is the period of stagnation. The following periods of accumulation and creativity are diminished as well.

Remember your teenage years? You were almost an adult, and you had more freedom. You could refuse to go to bed. You could read Harry Potter or party all night. Yeah!!! But what about the coming day? Most likely you didn't feel great. Too bad. The same thing happens to your soul when you resist the energy of lethargy.

Accept it and enjoy your lazy day. Something is brewing.

Plan for the week:
First thing in the morning when you look at yourself in the mirror:

- Look yourself in the eyes.
- Smile.
- Say: I love you.

Get your paper calendar and block 30 minutes for daily meditation in the morning for the next 7 days.

Block 10 minutes in the evening for contemplation.

Download the "Toxic Emotions: Lethargy" meditation.

Day 1–3:

> Use your downloaded guided meditation to learn how to accept and use lethargy—5–10 minutes.

Day 4–7:

> Meditate with lethargy on your own without listening to the guided meditation—30 minutes.

Try two other related meditations, melancholy and sadness, and see which one works best for you.

Use your evening contemplation time to assess your reactions to times when you felt like just stopping everything and lying in a hammock. If you feel painfully guilty, meditate with lethargy for a minute or two. Acknowledge your reaction again and see if it changes. Rate your emotion from zero to ten, where zero means you feel no remorse for calling in sick for no reason other than wanting to do nothing that day. Ten means you labor strenuously through the workweek and weekend to finish a one-paragraph blog and it still reads like gibberish.

13.3 Week 15: Grief

Pessimistic mind thinks that the loss of a parent, a spouse, a pet, or a job is a turning point towards the worst. Pessimistic mind refuses to be healed and carries grief as a memorial. Pessimistic mind is incapable of surviving, of starting a new chapter. Pessimistic mind is incapable of providing support to others.

Optimistic mind takes time to heal. It bravely creates a new future. Optimistic mind is capable of helping others. It will find the means to survive and gain wisdom.

We all carry grief. For the dead pet, for the lost love, for the lost parent. According to Ayurveda, the pericardium, the membrane enclosing the heart, is the organ responsible for processing all emotions. It is very resilient as it helps process the constant flow of pleasant and unpleasant emotions you experience during the day. When something very dear is taken from you, your body goes through very drastic energetic adjustments. You need the energy of grief to heal yourself.

When grief becomes too much, the pericardium might be weakened and stop processing. Marma points responsible for delivering Prana to your heart and lungs become blocked.

In 2003 the researcher Gordon Smith from Cambridge University published a paper in the *British Medical Journal* about the relationship between miscarriage and heart disease. He discovered that women who had experienced one miscarriage prior to the birth of their first child have a fifty (!) percent higher risk of heart disease. "Women with three or more early pregnancy losses were more than twice as likely to develop heart disease as women who had never had a miscarriage."[2] The biological mechanism of the relationship between miscarriage and heart disease is still poorly understood. But from the Ayurvedic point of view, this correlation makes perfect sense.

When marma points stop delivering Prana to organs, organs start to malfunction. Yes, you can die from a broken heart. When you learn to accept grief, you heal your heart, pericardium, and lungs. And you lead a happier, more fulfilling life. It is not easy. Grief is hard to accept.

My grandfather died in front of me when I was two and a half years old. I remember it vividly. There was a commotion the meaning of which I could not understand. My father taking me to my uncle's apartment.

---

[2] *Miscarriage and future maternal cardiovascular disease: a systematic review and meta-analysis, Clare Teresa Oliver-Williams, Emma E Heydon, Gordon C S Smith, Angela M Wood*

Three blissful and strange days I spent under the care of my aunt and elder cousins. I could play a piano; I could eat whatever I wanted, and the only thing that bothered me was that everyone was not very cheerful.

I don't remember much about the day I returned home except for my grandmother sitting on the balcony with her back to the door, my mother being "angry" at me, and everyone whispering. I knew they kept a secret. I just did not know what they were trying to keep from me.

When I asked about my grandfather, my parents did what the pediatrician told them to do—tell me that he went on a business trip, and no one knew when he would be coming home.

I don't remember when, but there was a point when I knew without asking that he was dead. And I appeared to be cool about this fact. I did not remember his face or his voice. He was not important in my life. But something changed.

We were all living together: my parents, my grandma, and me. Grandma and I shared a bedroom. I would wake up in the middle of the night to make sure she was breathing. One night I had an intense conversation with God. I demanded that he not take her from me. I offered God a deal: he could take as many years from my life as needed to add to her life. I made this pact with God when I was three.

Throughout my childhood no one understood why I was always so anxious when my mom went away on a business trip (which she did often). Waiting for her return was unbearable.

I grew up, went to college, became a software designer, and in 2007 followed my calling to become a Reiki Master and Teacher. Having an inquisitive mind, I was studying a lot of Ayurveda and Buddhist meditations. Buddhist meditations are very therapeutic, as they are developed to help to deal with emotional issues. I implemented many of these meditations in my practice.

When I was fifty, my husband of twenty-five years died in his sleep from a heart attack. I found him on the couch when I returned home from work. I was devastated. I was heartbroken. Well…. Doctor, heal thyself. I used all my tools to deal with the grief in the appropriate manner and help myself to heal and move forward with my life and take care of my child, my devastated parents-in-law, my parents, and my business.

Six months after his death I developed pneumonia. I went to the doctor to take care of it. But in my books, pneumonia is associated with unresolved grief. So I probably did not do such a good job after all. It had the potential to become a toxic emotion. I went to work on it without delay.

I started meditation to release grief. I recalled my husband's death to invoke grief. But it was not working. The memory of my very first dog popped up in my mind. I was unable even to say goodbye. She died in her sleep of old age and was buried without me. It was heartbreaking; we were young and grew up together. At that point I realized my grief was not about my husband. It was about not being able to say the last goodbye. And it was not about my husband or my dog. It was deep unresolved grief about my grandfather. The moment I started meditating about him, a person I thought I did not know well, the gates were opened. I wept, and wept, and wept. I was done. I released the grief that was poisoning me for years. Grief that made me so anxious when someone I love went on a business trip. Grief that made the wait so unbearable. All this was gone forever.

What came back were memories of my grandfather. The "stranger" at my birthday party beaming at my delight at having a toy horse now had the face of my grandfather. Some childhood memories I had did not make any sense. For example, why had my father, who was working at an engineering firm at that time, spent days at home with my grandmother caring for me, playing with me, laughing at my antics? It had not been my father after all. These memories became clearer and more well-defined with my grandfather's cheerful presence. And I also realized that my mother was not "angry" at me. She was heartbroken.

I was carrying grief for my grandfather for forty-eight years. Finally, I was healed. I was free.

Unprocessed grief can seriously impair your ability to process other emotions, lead to a lot of suffering, and weaken your abilities and natural gifts, because it takes a lot of energy to balance pain.

If you have experienced great loss in your life, you might find meditation with grief unbearable. Don't stop, however; don't give up. It is better to get it out of your system than to hold onto it. You don't do anyone any favors by holding onto grief. Your grief is not a memorial for the life lost; your love is.

Grief is the hardest emotion to work with. Take one day at a time. It is like being in the middle of a hurricane. Hold on. It will pass. And when it does, you will find yourself a much stronger, more compassionate person.

Plan for the week:
First thing in the morning when you look at yourself in the mirror:

- Look yourself in the eyes.
- Smile.
- Say: I love you.

Get your paper calendar and block 30 minutes for daily meditation in the morning for the next 7 days.

Block 10 minutes in the evening for contemplation.

Download the "Toxic Emotions: Grief" meditation.

Day 1–3:

> Use your downloaded guided meditation to learn how to accept and use grief—5-10 minutes.

Day 4–7:

> Meditate with grief on your own without listening to the guided meditation—30 minutes.

Try two other related meditations, melancholy and sadness, to see which one works best for you.

Use your evening contemplation time to gauge your reactions to sad events in your life or the lives of others. If some events make you cry or tear your heart apart, meditate with the grief caused by the event for a minute or two. Acknowledge your reaction again and see if it changes. Rate your emotion from zero to ten, where zero means you feel sadness for the loss but also joy for having this person or pet in your life. Ten means you cry inconsolably every time you see a couple holding hands or your neighbors walking a dog.

14

WHAT IS NEXT?

Congratulations! You made it. It was not an easy journey. I hope you feel better.

You did great. You have already learned useful time- and life-saving skills. You have developed habits for developing optimistic mind. And most importantly, you have learned to be aware of your mind and your emotions and are becoming a master of your mind. You are developing skills to turn any emotion into positive energy.

Keep practicing every day. Be aware of your experiences, emotions, and reactions. Download the meditations I provide for free to all my readers. Meditate. Meditate daily. The best time to meditate is in the morning and when you feel you don't have time to meditate. Nothing bad will happen if you spend five minutes of your busy day in quiet meditation and contemplation. But the impact you will make on yourself and others will be profound. You will approach conflicts calmly instead of over-emotionally. You will see the solutions instead of the problems. You will become a happier person instead of a miserable one. You will become free instead of being trapped by your own anger.

Don't give up. When you become aware of the blockage, start to dissolve it. And with proper emotional processing, you can achieve anything you want.

Don't worry too much when you don't progress quickly enough. You are not in a competition for sainthood. You just live your life. Life is not a test. For more guidance and inspiration, listen to my podcast:

https://anchor.fm/marina-lando

If you want more personal work, feel you need help processing emotions, or have a goal you want to work towards—such as finding a spouse, developing your career, or dealing with grief—sign up for a free 30-minute exploratory session (text Marina at: 919-469-1505) and see if the yearlong spiritual program "How to Train Optimistic Mind" might be right for you.

What happens next is under your full control. It is up to you, as you finish reading this last chapter, to make it the end of the book or the beginning of a long, fascinating journey.

ABOUT THE AUTHOR

Marina Lando

MS, Reiki Master Teacher, Aromatherapist, Published Author

For as long as she can remember, Marina has been passionate about making people well. She was first introduced to natural healing by her grandmother at about the age of 7. Marina's grandmother would take her to a forest or a meadow near her home and show her what to collect, how to find plants, how they smelled and felt, and how to use them. The family cupboard always smelled of dried flowers, and Linden tea is still Marina's first choice for a fever. When Marina had any pain, her grandmother would put her hand over Marina's body and the heat of her hands would soothe away the discomfort. Nobody called it Reiki, Medical Qi Gong, or any other exotic name. Marina just knew that her grandma was magic, and she wanted to be like her.

At the age of 9, Marina discovered the Children's Encyclopedia of Chemistry, and read it cover to cover, because she wanted to find a cure for her mom's migraines. She was amazed by the possibilities of mixing together chemicals and making drugs to cure diseases. At the same time, she was disappointed. It seemed that in many situations plants that her grandmother gathered every year provided just as much healing opportunity without as much hassle. So she did not become a chemist or a pharmacist, but she married a chemist (just in case).

Circumstances led Marina to earn Masters Degrees in both Computer Science and Economics. Later in life she learned Reiki, Ayurveda, and Aromatherapy professionally. She started her healing practice Harmony Life (HarmonyLifeReiki.com) in 2007. Marina continues to study and expand her knowledge, as there is always so much more to learn.

Marina lives in Cary, North Carolina, with her husband, Lola the cat, and Oscar the poodle. She is a black belt martial artist and an avid knitter.

How to connect with Marina:

Book appointment: HarmonyLifeReiki.com (in-person) 919-469-1505 (virtual)

Live Training:

> https://ahai.eventbrite.com

On-line Training:

> https://lando-medical-reiki-academy.thinkific.com/

Podcast:

> https://anchor.fm/marina-lando

Facebook:

> https://www.facebook.com/MarinaLandoReikiMaster/
> https://www.facebook.com/HarmonyLifeReiki/

Twitter:

> https://twitter.com/HarmonyLifeCary

LinkedIn:

> https://www.linkedin.com/in/marinalando/

Goodreads:

> https://www.goodreads.com/author/show/14769805.Marina_Lando

www.ingramcontent.com/pod-product-compliance
Lightning Source LLC
Chambersburg PA
CBHW060332130626
46553CB00003B/980